1900–1976

Geoff Stewart

Series Editor
Martin Collier

Heinemann

MANN ADVANCED HISTORY

Heinemann is an imprint of Pearson Education Limited, a company incorporated
in England and Wales, having its registered office at Edinburgh Gate, Harlow,
Essex, CM20 2JE. Registered company number: 872828

Heinemann is the registered trademark of
Pearson Education Limited

First published 2006

10
10 9 8 7

British Library Cataloguing in Publication Data is available
from the British Library on request.

ISBN: 9780435327699

Typeset by TechType, Abingdon, Oxon

Original illustrations © Harcourt Education Limited, 2006

Illustrated by TechType, Abingdon, Oxon

Cover photo: © Taxi/Getty

Printed in Hong Kong (EPC/07)

Acknowledgements

Every effort has been made to contact copyright holders of material reproduced in this book.
Any omissions will be rectified in subsequent printings if notice is given to the publishers.
Picture research by Jemma Street
(page 111) from Mao: The Unknown Story by Jung Chang, published by Jonathan Cape.
Reprinted by permission of The Random House Group Ltd (page 110) from The Private Life
of Chairman Mao by Zhisui Li, published by Chatto and Windus. Reprinted by permission
of the Random House Group Ltd; (page 111) Mao: A Life of Mao by Phlip Short (1999),
reproduced by permission of Hodder and Stoughton.
Photo credits: (Page 1) Art Directors and Trip; (Page 18) Getty Images/Hulton Archive;
(Page 38) Getty Images/Hulton Archive; (Page 47) Getty Images/Hulton Archive; (Page 59)
Getty Images/Hulton Archive; (Page 68) Corbis/Bettmann; (Page 77) Getty Images/Time Life
Pictures; (Page 94) Corbis/Bettmann; (Page 102) Corbis/Michael Maslan Historic Photographs;
(Page 124) ChinaStock; (Page 155) Getty Images/AFP; (Page 158) Corbis/Hulton-Deutsch
Collection; (Page 162) Corbis/Bettmann.

CONTENTS

HOW TO USE THIS BOOK

This is written as a simple text for any student studying the History of China between 1900 and 1976. The first chapter provides a basic introduction for students coming to Chinese history for the first time. It is important to get an outline of the geography of China, the high uplands of the west where the great rivers rise and the fertile lowlands of the east where most people live; also the differences between the hot semi tropical south and the more temperate north. Try to develop a sense of where the great cities of Beijing, Nanjing, Shanghai, Wuchang and Canton are; also where some of the more important provinces are in relation to one another. Chapters 2 to 6 deal with the collapse of the Qing Empire and the conflict and uncertainty that followed. Chapter 6 ends with the triumph of the Communists and the proclamation of the Peoples Republic of China in 1949. Chapters 7 to 12 cover the period of Communist rule down to Mao's death in 1976. Even if the period of study is only 1949–76, it is important to have read chapters 1 to 3, which try to explain some of the key aspects of Chinese history and civilisation and the origins and nature of the Chinese Communist Party. At the end of every chapter are 4 questions of the type asked at AS and the chapters should be read with these questions in mind. After reading a chapter, go back and identify which sections are relevant to the particular questions. Finally at the end is an assessment section, which tries to help in the construction of AS style answers. The bibliography is very basic, but the books mentioned there are accessible to AS students and most are very readable. There are of course thousands of more demanding academic texts, which can be consulted to assist in more detailed study.

CHAPTER I

There have been two methods
for rendering Chinese words
into western script: the
older **Wade–Giles** (W–G)
system – Peiching, Canton
(e.g. MaoTse tung), and
the system used today
– **Pinyin** (P), which is
favoured in China (e.g.
Bejing, Guangzhou and Mao
Zedong).

The **Qianlong (P)** or **Chien
Lung (W–G) Emperor**
was China's longest ruling
emperor (1736–99). Arguably
his reign was one of great
achievement and prosperity,
with a rapidly rising
population and conquest of
neighbouring territories.

Introduction

*As your Ambassador can see for himself, we possess all
things. I set no value in objects strange or ingenious, and
have no use for your country's manufactures.*

With these words directed to King George III, the great
Qianlong emperor bade farewell to Lord Macartney, the
first British ambassador to Beijing in 1793.

China's ruler, with some reason, felt himself to be the
centrepiece of a civilisation superior to any other in the
world. By the mid-eighteenth century, more books had
been published in Chinese than in all the other languages
of the world put together. The Emperor ruled over more
than 300 million subjects, 20 times more than those who
owed allegiance to King George. China was the world's
greatest producer of manufactured goods with some 33
per cent of the world total. Great Britain, the leading
European economy, produced just over 4 per cent.
Chinese porcelain had dazzled Europe since the
seventeenth century and
Europeans had only
recently learned the
secrets of its manufacture.
China at the time of the
Norman Conquest had
produced more iron than
England seven centuries
later. The first British
canal, completed in 1769,
was insignificant
compared to the 1,000-
mile Grand Canal linking
the Yangtze and Hwang
Ho Rivers, and this had
been built in the seventh
century.

The Yangtze Gorge

Yet it was not only Chinese material achievements that gave rise to self-confidence and a sense of superiority. As a later British visitor to China, Sir Robert Hart, was to write in 1901: *'In no other country is education so prized.'*

The empire was governed by scholar civil servants, selected by a complex examination system which had been in operation for over a thousand years. English civil servants were not selected by examination till 1871. A complex and efficient postal system carried the Emperor's orders and his scholar officials' frequent reports across the thousands of miles of his realm. Chains of post horses ensured that official letters travelled up to 250 miles a day. In 1759 and 1792, the Qianlong Emperor had extended his effective authority into the barren uplands of Tibet and Xinjiang with superbly organised military expeditions. The borders of modern China had been established.

Mountains, rivers and cities

THE IMPORTANCE OF CLIMATE AND TRADE

At the other end of the giant northern landmass to Europe, China was and is a remarkable triumph of human ingenuity. On 7 per cent of the world's farmland, 20 per cent of the world's population is fed. Most live and have lived in the low-lying waterlands of the mighty Yangtze and Yellow Rivers. These have been the source of life and also frequent death. Rising in the high uplands of central Asia, they flow for more than 3,000 miles down to the Yellow Sea.

The Yellow River in particular has been unpredictable and vicious in its flooding and changes of course. Thousands died in the 1850s when it dramatically changed its exit point into the sea, some 200 miles north of its old delta. Yet the rivers not only supply water for irrigation but also transport, the Yangtze being navigable from the great port of Shanghai at its mouth for 1,400 miles upstream through the cities of Nanjing and Wuhan.

The range of climate matches the size of the country and the consequent range of products and food make Chinese cuisine the complex joy that many in the west have come to appreciate. In the north, along the Yellow River, wheat and millet prevail and the icy winds from Mongolia produce freezing winters. Nevertheless, warm summers enable the production of cotton, all manner of fruits and soya beans. It is around the Yangtze and to the south that China's lush fertile heart beats strongest. Rice feeds the teeming millions, but the ever-present ponds, streams and lakes are filled with fish and ducks. Mulberry trees provide food for silk worms, and silk became one of the manufactured glories of China. Tea, and further south, sugar cane abound. It was to the southern ports of Macao and Canton that foreigners first came and found there was a treasure trove of goods to take back to Europe. The problem was what to sell the Chinese in exchange.

THE CHINESE DYNASTIES

Nature, through climate and water, had in part made all this abundance possible, but it was also the way the Chinese people had organised themselves and the values that infused their society that had held them together for so long. Traditionally, Chinese history is divided into dynastic periods (see the timeline) going back to the mysterious Xia Dynasty around 2000 BC. Their successors were the Shang Dynasty and it was at the site of their capital city of Anyang, near to the Yellow River, that evidence of the first Chinese writing appears. Shang gave way to Zhou around 1000 BC, and about this time the important and persistent concept of the **Mandate of Heaven** emerged to justify the overthrow of the last tyrant Shang ruler.

Confucius and Mencius

It was some 500 years later at a time of chaos and warfare, as the Zhou dynasty lost control, that the sage, Kong Qui, known to the west as **Confucius**, lived. It could be argued that his ideas have dominated China ever since. Roughly contemporary with Socrates in Greece and the Buddha in India, it is remarkable that at the same time in completely separate human societies, three great minds functioned and left a moral, social and intellectual legacy that has endured for 2,500 years. Confucius had his thoughts recorded in a book known as the *Analects*.

Confucian ideas were later expanded upon and developed by another sage, known in the west as **Mencius**, or **Meng Tzu** or Meng K'o. Meng Tzu defended the ideas of Confucius against critics and his ideas are recorded in a text known as the *Mencius*. Both texts later became key elements of study for scholars wishing to take the examination which gave those who were successful access to the senior posts in government.

The texts became the philosophy and approach to life underpinning the Chinese state and civilisation. Harmony and decorum could be achieved by correct behaviour, which could be ascertained by reason. Respect for legitimate authority, that of a parent, an older brother or a government enjoying the Mandate of Heaven was crucial. Courtesy should be shown one to another and war and chaos at all levels were abominations. Dynasties gained and kept power by showing humanity and righteousness. They lost authority when they failed to show these qualities, becoming tyrants. The way of Confucius was embodied in the old Chinese saying, 'Reform yourself, then arrange your family and so pacify

The **Mandate of Heaven** is the phrase used to justify the authority of an Emperor and his Dynasty. They were the key link between human society and nature. The good fortune of a conqueror was seen as conferring the mandate, but his evil actions and abuse of power could be interpreted as bringing about the loss of the Mandate of Heaven. This was often revealed in some natural disaster such as a flood or famine.

Confucius (470–391 BC) and Meng Tzu (372–289 BC) were the two writers who put into words, during the dying years of the Zhou Dynasty, an approach to life that dominated the Chinese state until the twentieth century.

Universal Mirror to Aid Government was a chronicle of Chinese history from 403 BC to AD 959 compiled under the Song Dynasty in the eleventh century. Mao read it over and over again going through its 9,612 pages in the last year of his life for the eighteenth time.

KEY TERM

Feng Shui is a popular Chinese concept in which good fortune and happiness is induced by the 'correct' placing of buildings and even articles within the building.

KEY TERM

Legalism relied on an uncompromising system of rewards and punishments and offered a contrasting moral code to that of Confucius.

KEY TERMS

The **Great Wall** is a massive structure in the north of China, running from just north of Beijing over 1,000 miles westwards, to protect the settled farming lands of the Yellow River valley from raiding barbarian nomads. Sections were begun before the Qin and Han, but in its present form much is the work of the Ming Dynasty who began a massive strengthening of it in 1474.

the world'. Harmony was desirable in all things. **Feng Shui** seeks to do this for places; Chinese cooking seeks harmony through the opposites of sweet and sour. There was a belief in the interconnectedness of all things, and the righteous ruler was essential in maintaining harmony in nature. A natural catastrophe could be blamed on the incorrect behaviour of the sovereign and often signalled the removal of the Mandate of Heaven from a dynasty.

The way of Confucius did not concern itself with the supernatural or an afterlife although it was far from denying these. Its concern was with the ordering of human society and the production on Earth of a heavenly harmony, often symbolised through music and ritual. Religious philosophies which did address the supernatural were to flourish in China, most notably in the form of Daoism and later in Buddhism, imported from India. Despite considerable influence at different times and in particular parts of China, neither really threatened the dominating Confucian code.

The Qin and Han Dynasties

Sixty years after the death of Mencius, China was reunited under the Chin or Qin Dynasty, from which the very name China comes. The unification was to last, but not the dynasty. The first emperor of Qin (Shi Huangdi) has left a fabulous memorial to his power in what is now one of the great tourist attractions of the modern world. Seven thousand terracotta, life-size soldiers were created and then entombed to guard the emperor in the after-life, and the workers who created the tomb were buried with the Emperor's corpse to keep the secret of his grave. He was also responsible for beginning that other wonder of China, the **Great Wall**. The first Qin Emperor ruled, not according to the Confucian code, but with a harsh brutality that was known in China as **Legalism**, that is, obey or face the consequences. The Emperor was to be one of Mao Zedong's heroes. Yet his dynasty did not last, collapsing in 206 BC following widespread rebellion.

It was a peasant who in 202 BC gained the Mandate of Heaven, becoming the Emperor GaoZu and founding the long-lasting Han Dynasty. Under him, the Great Wall was extended and government, increasingly influenced by Confucian scholars, evolved into a complex and sophisticated system, comparable to that of the contemporary Roman Empire. Individual Emperors might prefer the techniques of the Legalist school, such as the long reigning WuDi (141–87 BC), who, while employing more and more Confucian scholars, had a habit of boiling alive those who crossed him. The leading historian of his reign was castrated for defending a general who was out of favour with the Emperor. It is worth remembering that sophisticated, bureaucratic government went hand in hand with an arbitrary brutality. Mao and other educated Chinese of the twentieth century were well acquainted with the detailed history of the Qin and Han Dynasties, as well as the later dynasties, and much influenced by them.

Disunion and the Tang Dynasty

From approximately AD 200, there was another period of warring states, which ended when China was reunited under the Sui Dynasty in the sixth century. Despite these interludes, there was real continuity in China's history, unlike Europe over a similar time span. It is as if the Roman Empire had never fully collapsed but after periods of difficulty re-emerged stronger than ever. There was nothing comparable to the so-called Dark Ages of western Europe in the fifth and sixth centuries when learning, and even the coinage, seems to have all but disappeared. In China it was a period of inventiveness. Block printing developed and the use of the first paper money. The Sui soon gave way to first the Tang and then the Song Dynasty in the tenth century. By this time, most of the forms and structures of government, which were to last until 1905/1911, were in place. Under the Emperor, the country was to be governed by scholar officials selected by examination.

Candidates were tested on the Confucian classic texts and had to demonstrate a mastery not only of the ideas of Confucius and Mencius but also a mastery of calligraphy. Examinations were held, first locally for entry to the lowest grade of scholar, then at provincial level to secure the possibility of a post of magistrate or junior bureaucrat. Finally, to achieve the prestigious Jinshi degree, giving access to the highest offices in the state, candidates had to take a series of demanding tests in the capital. In theory, the system gave the empire the best men to govern and it

An example of Chinese calligraphy

was possible for the poor man to rise to the pinnacle of power and prestige through learning. In practice, the complexities of Chinese writing, which took years to master, limited selection to the wealthy gentry families who could afford to support an unproductive member of the family for years while studying. The complex brushstrokes in writing the characters became an art form in itself. In the hands of an expert it was and is capable of great sensitivity and complex nuances. Despite the demands of mastering the written language, literacy in China was consistently higher than in Europe before the 20th century.

The written language not directly related to the spoken language gave unity to a vast country with many different languages and dialects. Written Chinese was the essential glue holding the state together.

The Song Dynasty

It was during the Song period that the practice of binding the feet of young girls, after first breaking the bones, emerged. This ensured that the feet did not grow but remained a dainty 3 inches (7.5 cm) and as such a much sought-after attribute of female beauty. Originally only used among female performers and courtesans, it became common among all families with any social aspiration. Over the centuries, despite the intense pain inflicted, the custom spread down the social ladder. Chinese men reputedly found women with large feet, i.e. normal size, repulsive. Foot-binding symbolised the second-class position of women in China. The male side of the family was all-important. On marriage, a girl had to forsake her own family and her prime obligation and obedience was to her husband and her husband's parents, not her own. There was, and is, a complete difference for a child between the esteem in which an uncle on the father's side of the family is held and the relationship with the mother's brothers. There is no one word for 'uncle' as in English and jiujiu, a mother's brother is far less important than shushu, a father's younger brother, let alone bobo, a father's elder brother.

Mongol rule

The Song Dynasty, like many others, collapsed under attacks from barbarians beyond the Great Wall. First the

Jurchin or Jin (from Manchuria) drove the Song from the Yellow River valley cities; then, in the thirteenth century, the Mongols destroyed both the Jin and the Song Dynasties, establishing a reunited China under Kubilai Khan (great grandson of Ghenghis). This took the name of the Yuan Dynasty. For the first time, direct contact via the Silk Road was established with Europe and Europeans reached China, the most famous, because of his memoirs, being the Italian **Marco Polo**. There could be little doubt at this time where the most developed part of the world was. Chinese cities dwarfed those of Europe and their technology made Europeans appear as intellectual pygmies. The ease and luxury of Chinese urban life delighted Marco Polo. Here was a world of restaurants, show business and the printed novel, although the literary sophistication of China was of the least interest to the young Italian.

The Ming and Qing Dynasties

The Yuan Dynasty of Kubilai did not last and, in 1368, the Mongols were chased out to their native steppes to the west, and a native Chinese dynasty, drawn from the **Han,** took over to rule as the Ming Dynasty. Early in the years of their rule one of the great potential turning points in world history took place. The Yongle emperor dispatched a series of naval forces, between 1405 and 1421, to explore southwards and westwards across the Indian Ocean. Under the eunuch admiral Zheng He, India, the Gulf States of Arabia and the east coast of Africa were reached. It has been argued that they penetrated even further into the Atlantic. After the emperor's death, the voyages were discontinued and the large ships left to rot. Had they continued there is little doubt that the Chinese would have discovered Europe, considerably before the Portuguese reached China in 1514. Instead of a Chinese mandarin stepping ashore, as the representative of the Son of Heaven in Lisbon or London, and exciting the wonder of Europeans, it was Tomes Pires, who arrived as ambassador for Portugal in 1517 and was allowed after some delay to travel to Beijing.

In the seventeenth century, once again the Mandate of Heaven was withdrawn. Natural disasters and plague indicated the Ming as unfit to govern and conquerors

KEY PERSON

Marco Polo (1254–1324) is of interest not because he was the first European to visit China which he wasn't but because his memoirs, written as a prisoner in Genoa, made him the best known visitor to China and created a sensation. Much of his book seemed at the time nothing but tall stories. Much of the geography is muddled. Some scholars suggest that he never reached China. The memoirs are a fascinating way of comparing two contemporary societies.

KEY TERM

Han is the name used by themselves to describe the overwhelming majority of the people of China and to distinguish themselves from the minority nationalities such as the Tibetans of the west or the Manchus of the north.

from the north, the Manchus, seized the empire and established a new dynasty, the Qing. Like the Mongols before them, the conquerors adopted many of the ways of the conquered, including their system of government by scholar bureaucrats. Yet there were things they refused to accept and Manchu women were ordered not to bind their feet, a trait which rendered them sexually repellent to most Han Chinese. As a symbol of their lordship over China, all Chinese men were ordered to shave the front of their heads and wear their hair in a pigtail. This badge of servitude lasted until 1911.

Yet under the Qing, China prospered. The population doubled between the mid-seventeenth and mid-eighteenth centuries. Under the three great emperors, Kangxi (1661–1723), Yongzheng (1723–36) and Qianlong (1736–99), China appeared as the sun at midday – at the height of power. Great military expeditions were efficiently organised to bring Tibet and the far western province of Xinkiang under control. There was nothing to gain from, let alone fear, aliens like the British and their strange ambassador Lord Macartney who refused to make the ritual **kowtow** to the Emperor.

Signs of decline

But much had changed since the days of Marco Polo. In terms of technology, Europe now appeared to be the growing point of humanity. As the Grand Canal silted up, the British were building canals to link their new industrial cities. Iron production in Britain far exceeded China and the great Chinese iron production centres of the past in Hopei had closed.

The population possibly tripled between 1680 and the end of the eighteenth century. Initially, this was simply making good the population losses brought about by plague and war in the seventeenth century. Later, new lands were brought under cultivation and new crops like sweet potatoes and peanuts fed more people. But trouble was building. In the fertile lowlands, family holdings became smaller as under Chinese law of inheritance the land was shared out among all male children. Around Beijing, the average holding by 1800 was just over a hectare. In the upland new areas forests were cleared and

KEY TERM

Kowtow was the ritual way of approaching the emperor, crawling on hands and knees and touching the floor with the forehead.

initially good crops resulted from the virgin soil. The deforestation, however, produced a more rapid run-off of water, contributing to the disastrous floods of the nineteenth century. Chinese farmers traditionally relied on human excrement to replenish the soil. In the new areas this was not available in sufficient quantity. Soil impoverishment was the result, and from this, increasing famine resulted. China, on a far vaster scale, faced the problems of Ireland, in the same period. The demographic crisis was bound eventually to lead to a social and political crisis.

In science and medicine, China once so superior to the west, was slipping behind. In 1793, the Emperor Qianlong's favourite, He Shen, and the most powerful official in the Empire, was plagued by pains and illness. His Chinese doctors blamed a spirit which shifted from place to place in his flesh. Macartney's Scottish doctor, Hugh Gillan, put it down to rheumatism and a serious hernia. He recommended a truss.

CONCLUSION

There could be little doubt in the minds of the few European visitors to China that they were encountering a very old and impressive civilisation. Its cities still dwarfed those of Europe and the range of its products still hinted at fabled wealth. Contacts, still largely limited to Canton in the south, encouraged an air of mystery and romance and hid the very real weaknesses which over the next hundred years were to become all too apparent.

SUMMARY QUESTIONS

1 In what ways did the physical geography of China make possible extensive food production and commerce?

2 In what ways did Chinese writing and Confucian Ideas help to maintain the unity of China?

3 Which social customs indicated the inferior status of women in China?

4 In what ways might Qing China in the eighteenth century be regarded as a successful and impressive state?

DYNASTIC TIMELINE

Xia c2200–1750 BC

Shang c1600–c1100 BC

Zhou c1100–256 BC

Qin c221–206 BC

Han c202 BC–AD 220

Period of Disunion c220–589

Sui 589–618

Tang 618–960

Period of Disunion 907–960

Song 960–1127

Jin in north and Song in South 1127–1234

Yuan 1279–1368

Ming 1368–1644

Qing 1644–1912

CHAPTER 2

The last years and fall of the Qing Dynasty

INTRODUCTION

On 12th February 1912, the six-year old Xuantung Emperor, whose personal name was Puyi, peacefully abdicated, surrendering the throne of his ancestors. China became a republic. In theory, it was the end of Imperial China. In both theory and reality, it was the end of the Qing Dynasty which had ruled since 1644. Like most important events it was the product of a complex mix of circumstances and deep-seated causes. Very few Chinese doubted that the dynasty had lost the Mandate of Heaven.

THE IMPACT OF THE WEST

Nationalist Chinese writers and even some Western historians have often stressed as the prime cause of decline the humiliations heaped on China by the European powers and Japan. The starting point for this is usually taken to be the so-called **Opium War** with Britain in 1839–42. Lord Macartney's embassy had asked for extended trading rights and permanent representation in Beijing by a British diplomat; in other words, the setting up of an embassy. All his demands were rejected. China and her officials had no sense of equality between nations. There was the Son of Heaven in Beijing and there were tributary states. They could see no point in a permanent British diplomatic representative. Until 1815, Britain was too busy with the French Revolution and Napoleon to take the matter further. In 1816, a second mission was dispatched to Beijing. Britain as in 1793 was in keen competition with Dutch merchants from the Dutch East Indies. It was not even received. Trade remained limited to Canton and had to be conducted through a group of thirteen licensed merchants, the Cohong.

There were also disputes over the application of Chinese law to foreigners. The principles and practice of law in the Chinese Empire seemed very different from that of Europe. In 1784, a British sailor who had accidentally

KEY EVENT

The **Opium War** was a clear demonstration of how weak China had become *vis à vis* the advanced nations of Europe. Sporadic fighting began around Canton in 1839, but the main British fleet did not arrive till June 1840. Instead of attacking Canton, it moved north to the mouth of the Yangtze and then north to the Dagu forts guarding the approaches to Tiajin and Beijing. Negotiations began and a compromise peace was arranged which was rejected by both British Foreign Minister Palmerston and the Emperor. Fresh British reinforcements arrived from India in 1842 and Shanghai was captured and Nanjing threatened. This produced peace on British terms.

killed a Chinese boatman in firing a salute had been handed over to the Chinese authorities for justice and had been strangled. The memory of this still rankled on British ships and among British merchants and sailors.

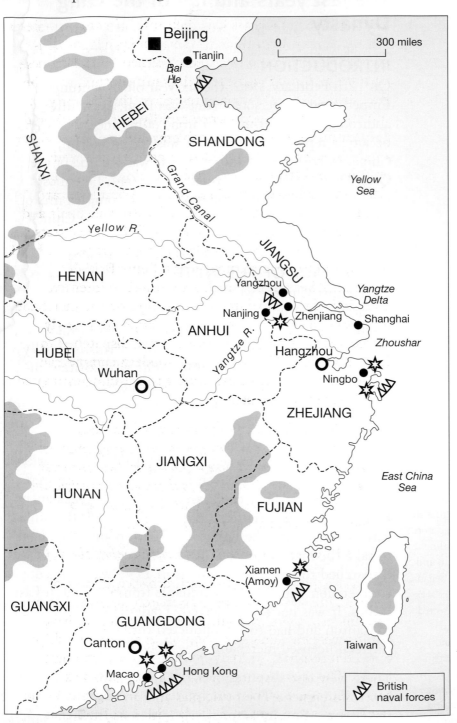

The Opium War, 1839–42

The British were anxious to extend their trade and force China into what they saw as a more modern and open relationship. By the 1830s, the British Foreign Secretary, Lord Palmerston, was prepared for tough action.

The Chinese authorities had their own growing problems arising from foreign trade. Imports of opium for non-medical use had been repeatedly banned by the Chinese authorities throughout the eighteenth century, and the British East India Company respected this but private traders did not. Imports grew rapidly in the 1820s and 1830s causing both social problems and a drain of silver. In 1838, the Emperor decided to prohibit the trade in opium. He dispatched the jinshi holding official, Lin Zexu, to implement it. Three million pounds of raw opium were seized in 1839. Mixed with water, salt and lime, they were flushed into the sea. What the effects on marine life were is not recorded, but prayers were offered urging all creatures to move away. Some British merchants were imprisoned. As a result of intensive lobbying of the government in London by the merchants in Canton, an expedition of 16 warships, four newly armed steamers and 4,000 troops were dispatched to Canton to make China enter the modern commercial world. Initially, the Chinese ruling elite underestimated the power of the British:

> *The English barbarians are an insignificant and detestable race, trusting entirely to their strong ships and large guns: but the immense distance they have traversed will render the arrival of seasonal supplies impossible and their soldiers after a single defeat, being deprived of provisions will become dispirited and lost.*

> *(A mandarin's report to the Emperor before the conflict)*

The war exposed the technological backwardness of China. Their war junks were no match for armed steamers and modern cannon. Monkeys armed with primitive bombs were encouraged to hop on to the British ships but often returned to their Chinese hosts with bombs intact. The banning of the export of rhubarb was conceived as a war winning strategy, the Chinese being under the impression that the British had a fatal propensity to constipation. This did not bring Britain to her knees and, in June 1842, the British captured Shanghai and then moved up the Yangtze halting all traffic on the Grand Canal. The result was the humiliating Treaty of Nanjing. Five Chinese cities, including Shanghai, were to be open to British merchants and Hong Kong Island was to be transferred to the sovereignty of the British crown. China agreed to pay compensation for damages suffered by British merchants and to accept Britain as an equal in terms of diplomacy.

In 1844 the Americans and the French extracted new treaties extending their trading rights. Shanghai became a symbol of the new relationship with a rapid expansion of trade and a thriving foreign community of merchants, particularly British. Here they created, at the centre of a Chinese community, a part of England, with an Anglican Church and an English Public School. In 1855, 437 foreign ships entered the port and the numbers continued to grow.

The second Anglo-Chinese War

Fresh conflicts continued to grow. The British attempted to extend commercial access, particularly inland up the Yangtze. Piracy and law and order remained an issue and the original demand of Lord Macartney for a permanent ambassador in Beijing had not been met. The chance to press these aims came late in 1856, following the **Arrow incident**. This time the British struck close to Beijing seizing the Dagu Forts and threatening to take the strategic port and city of Tianjin. A fresh treaty was conceded by the Emperor's representative official, giving the British most of what they wanted. It amounted to an abandonment of Chinese sovereignty over various ports as British warships could enter any Chinese port in pursuit of pirates. Symbolically, the Qing Emperor was to receive a British ambassador in Beijing and stop using the character (yi) to describe the British. 'Yi' meant alien. This was too much for the Emperor who refused to ratify the treaty. After further hard fighting and initial defeat, a British force reinforced by the French, marched on Beijing. The Emperor's summer palace in the suburbs of the city was burned down. The Emperor, duly chastened, now accepted the 1858 treaty with even greater concessions than in the original **Treaty of Tianjin**. A

The **Arrow incident** was the seizure by the Chinese authorities in Canton of a vessel registered in Hong Kong, and therefore technically British. In reality, its registration documents were out of date and the Chinese Mandarin responsible was in the right. This did not stop the new British government of Lord Palmerston pressing the quarrel and, when defeated in the House of Commons on a debate, holding and winning a general election. The British public approved of a vigorous policy and the Mandarin was seized and exiled to India.

KEY EVENT

The Treaty of Tianjin (1858/60)

allowed the establishment of western embassies in the capital, gave the British access up the Yangtze to Hankow and allowed missionaries and others the opportunity to travel freely.

contemporary British comment makes clear the importance of the war and the subsequent treaty:

> *By this war we have practically opened out the trade of the Yangtze River, whence a vastly increased commerce is to be expected. We have inflicted a severe blow upon the pride of the Hsien–feng Emperor that the whole face of Chinese politics and our relations with that country must change, before he will dare insult our flag or obstruct our commerce.*

(Lt Col G J Wolseley)

One result of this second Anglo-Chinese War was the establishment of a Chinese foreign ministry, the Zongli Yamen, dominated by the Emperor's uncle, Prince Gong.

By the 1860s, the influence of foreigners began to increase as contact between them and the Chinese elite and Chinese merchants increased. There was an increasing need to learn foreign languages and language schools were opened in many of the major ports. In Beijing the original language school developed into a fully fledged western-style college in 1867. Such developments inevitably excited opposition. One mandarin argued that the contemporary drought was a direct result of the

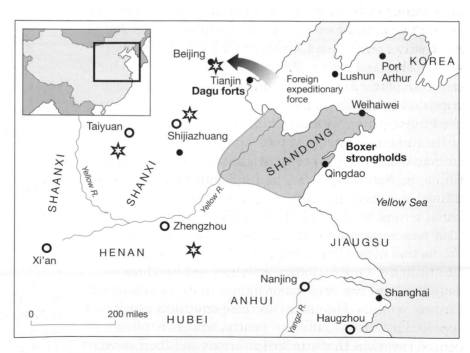

Boxer rising and foreign response

opening of the new college. Heaven was showing its disapproval.

The establishment of missionaries

Perhaps the greatest resentment was directed against missionaries, whose scale of operations had been extended by the treaty of 1860, which gave them freedom to travel throughout the Empire. They and their converts were often persecuted and sometimes killed. Besides many Catholic missionaries who looked to France for protection, there were many Protestant ones from Britain and the USA. These Christians displayed a tendency to baptise children and in particular sick and dying children, of which there were many. The burial of these led to a widespread belief that Christians used body parts in witchcraft. Small corpses were dug up from Christian burial grounds and used to demonstrate the wickedness of the west. It was against the Catholics who had built a large church in Tianjin that one of the most dramatic of anti-Christian outbursts took place. Sixteen French missionaries including ten nuns, who were first stripped, were killed by an angry crowd in 1870. The French government demanded punishment of the guilty and 16 Chinese were duly executed by the Chinese authorities.

This was no more than a small hiccup in the process. The missionaries continued to pour in, opening schools and, most welcomed by the Chinese at all levels, hospitals. Missionaries and their schools were to have considerable influence on the China of the twentieth century. Chinese pupils often became imbued with western ideas and the need to promote reform in China. Charlie Soong was one of the most successful of young Chinese men who embraced the west and western ideas. Born in southern China, he went to the USA in 1878 and, after various jobs, trained as a missionary and returned to China in 1886. He found selling bibles to other missionaries more profitable than preaching and from this, and later the factory production of noodles, made a fortune. He used part of his wealth to fund revolutionary activities and his three daughters and son were major figures in twentieth-century Chinese politics. The enemy to these reformers usually appeared to be the Confucian gentry, who were often behind the mobs that attacked missions and their converts.

Tributary status The Chinese emperors had long claimed a general over-lordship with regard to North Vietnam and Korea. While being left for the most part to govern themselves, their rulers on accession sent gifts to Beijing and sought approval of their rule.

THE LOSS OF THE TRIBUTARY STATES

A further clash with France developed in the 1880s, over the French consolidation of its hold on Vietnam. Traditionally, Vietnam like Korea occupied a **tributary status** with regard to Imperial China. The rulers of both Vietnam in the south and Korea in the north recognised the lordship if not the direct rule of the Emperor in Beijing. The French brutally severed any link, destroying a Chinese fleet in Fuzhou in August 1884, in the process. Five Frenchmen and 521 Chinese men died.

In 1894 Qing China suffered a serious humiliation over the other tributary state, Korea, and this time at the hands of an Asiatic power, Japan. Japan, newly reformed and invigorated, was anxious to extend its influence into Korea at China's expense. A rebellion in Korea against the monarchy there led both powers to rush in troops.

A ship carrying Chinese reinforcements was sunk by a Japanese cruiser and for good measure Japanese forces crossed into Chinese territory proper, seizing the port of Lushun in Manchuria and even the Shandong peninsula near to Beijing itself. The Treaty of Shimoneseki was more humiliating than that of Nanjing in 1842. China abandoned Korea and even ports in China to Japan. The treaty elicited protests from the elite. Gathered in Beijing for the prestigious Jinshi examination, China's most brilliant Confucian scholars demonstrated against the treaty and demanded reform. The Qing Dynasty was beginning to totter.

LOSS OF SOVEREIGNTY AND THE BOXER RISING

In 1898 and 1899, China almost seemed on the point of partition between the imperialist powers. The Russians who had forced the Japanese out of some of their gains, notably the port of Lushun, now occupied much of Manchuria and Lushun, renaming it Port Arthur. The Germans occupied a port in the Shandong peninsula and the British, not to be outdone and to stop anyone else having it took Weihaiwei. They also extended their hold on the south by extracting a 99-year lease on the Kowloon Peninsula to the north of Hong Kong. The French also seized territory in the south. The Qing government seemed helpless and unable to defend Chinese sovereignty.

In this situation, popular feeling in north-east China erupted into what became known as the **Boxer Rising**. Tension had been growing for some time over western missionaries and their Christian converts. In the spring of 1900 isolated incidents coalesced into a mass frenzy of anti-western outrage. It was fuelled by a mixture of primitive magical beliefs and outraged Han pride. Railways which were spreading in the north were thought to disturb dragons, and telegraph wires which dripped rusty water after rain were regarded as sources of poison. Europeans and even those Chinese in possession of dangerous foreign objects such as clocks were killed. Such events were to be repeated during the Cultural Revolution of 1966, which was marked by similar xenophobic lunacy.

Mobs from the countryside spread to Tianjin and Beijing. The German ambassador was shot and Europeans retreated to the British legation (embassy) to withstand a siege. The Empress Dowager Cixi in control of the Qing court threw her support behind the Boxers, in effect declaring war on the west. It was popular but hopeless. In August 1900, an international force advanced on Beijing and relieved the legation. The Qing court fled to Xi'an far to the west, leaving the veteran mandarin Li Hongzhang to negotiate peace. Massive damages were extracted, which amounted to nearly twice the annual revenue of the state. Here was a crippling burden comparable to the reparations later to be heaped on Germany at the end of the First World War and, like those forced payments, these on China produced a similar reaction of outraged bitterness and nationalism.

> ## KEY EVENT
>
> The **Boxer Rising (1900)** took its name from the participants' self-adopted name – the Boxers United in Righteousness. Many were members of secret societies practising martial arts. Its ranks were largely filled with poor young peasants. There were some women among them known as the Red Lanterns Shining.

The Empress Dowager Cixi

THE NATIONALIST BACKLASH

Sixty years of repeated defeats had elicited an incoherent and doomed protest in the form of the Boxer Rising. In the early years of the twentieth century, they began to bring about a genuine nationalist movement among the educated elite, which was to be the driving force of change throughout twentieth-century China. Initially, hostility to the west among some of the educated Confucian gentry was an ostrich-like ignoring of all things western, but others came to see that this was a recipe for further humiliations. Japan provided a model of a more effective way to react. Japan had been forced to open her doors to western traders in the 1850s. In 1867–68, this shock produced a transformation in these islands lying so close to the Chinese mainland. The Meji Emperor became the figure-head for reform. The only way to compete with and survive the western challenge was to embrace western technology and various aspects of western government and society. The Japanese took what they perceived to be the most powerful European models. Their army was to be like that of Prussia, their navy modelled on Britain. Yet change was wrapped in a conservative garb headed by the venerable figure of the Emperor, who, it was claimed, was now restored to power in place of the Shogun. For China, the deadly fall-out of this process was the brutal defeat in Korea in 1894. Japan had joined the ranks of the predators.

Increasingly, many younger members of the scholar-gentry class drew the conclusion that China should take Japan's path of reform. One of the youngest and most strident was **Zou Rong**. He had studied in Japan and came to believe that only with the destruction of the Qing Dynasty could China be saved. He appealed in a book, *The Revolutionary Army*, published in 1903, to Han resentment of the ruling Manchu and detestation of the western 'foreign devils'. His book was used and distributed widely by an even more famous nationalist, **Sun Yat-sen.** Like many Chinese nationalists, Sun had spent much time abroad. Such years in exile led to reflection on Qing China and also a heightened sense of what it was to be Chinese.

KEY PEOPLE

Zou Rong (1885–1905)
was a remarkably influential figure for one so young. He published his book *The Revolutionary Army* at 18 and died in prison just before his twentieth birthday.

There was a growing number of nationalist protests in the first decade of the twentieth century. There were protests against the Russians in Mongolia and Manchuria, against the latest threat from the British in Tibet and, most dramatic of all, extensive outrage at US immigration restrictions and mistreatment of Chinese visitors to the World Fair in St. Louis. In June 1905, this outrage led to the declaration of a total boycott of American goods by Chinese merchants in many of the most important ports. It was to last until September.

The attitude to Japan was one of ambivalence, particularly after 1905, when for the first time an Asiatic country inflicted defeat on a European power. Japan's victory over Russia in that year, in particular at the former Chinese port of Lushun (Port Arthur), sent a pleasant shiver of anticipation through the politically conscious young in China. If Japan could do it, perhaps China could do it to her tormentors, if she fully embraced reform. Thousands flocked to Japan for education. One of these was so outraged by a photograph he saw there of the execution in 1894 of a Chinese prisoner that he gave up the study of medicine to devote himself to the transformation of China. His pen name was **Lu Xun**.

THE INTERNAL CRISIS IN CHINA

Even without foreign pressure and humiliation, China faced growing and probably insoluble internal problems. At the root of these lay the population explosion of the eighteenth century (see Chapter 1, page 9).

A further economic crisis developed from the growing addiction to opium and its purchase from foreigners. Apart from the social damage, serious economic problems developed as a result of the out-flow of silver from China (9 million taels per annum by the 1830s). This produced a serious silver shortage which damaged internal commerce.

The last years of the Qianlong emperor also saw mounting corruption on the part of officials. At the centre was the Emperor's favourite, He Shen, who took bribes on a massive scale, skimming off his take from other officials who then replicated the process with their juniors. It spread down the hierarchy to the lowest village

Sun Yat-sen (1866–1925) is considered by many as the father figure of modern China. He trained as a doctor in Hong Kong and then became involved in anti-Qing activities, trying to promote a revolt in 1895. He fled to Europe and was kidnapped in London by the Imperial Chinese government. In 1905, he organised the Revolutionary Alliance devoted to the overthrow of the Qing and the establishment of a republic. He became a hero to radical Chinese reformers. He was partly funded by Charlie Soong, whose daughter he married.

KEY PERSON

Lu Xun (1881–1936) is generally considered the most important Chinese writer of the twentieth century. He devoted himself to satirising traditional Chinese culture. His first book, *Diary of a Madman*, was published in 1918. He never joined the Communist Party but was held in high regard and was praised by Mao Zedong.

and town level. When the Qianlong emperor died in 1799, his successor forced He Shen to commit suicide. He was found to be holding millions of taels of silver, equivalent to two years' revenue of the entire realm. Despite his death, corruption remained endemic, and the central government failed to extract the taxes that its predecessors had been able to do. This was to be a serious weakness in resisting the challenges of foreigners.

Rebellions of the nineteenth century

Population pressure, governmental financial weakness and corruption came together to produce a series of spectacular rebellions against the Qing authority. Traditionally, this had always been a sign of dynasties losing the Mandate of Heaven. The problem was present in the latter years of the Qianlong emperor, facing what became known as the White Lotus Rebellion between 1796 and 1804. Like so many such rebellions, it was partly inspired by religious mysticism, in this case Buddhist. It clearly exposed weaknesses in the Qing state costing a hundred million taels to suppress, and showing the incapacities of the military organisation.

The greatest of all the rebellions was the **Taiping Rebellion** of 1851–64, which threatened the very existence of the Qing Empire. Like so many would-be revolutionaries in all countries, its founder and leader, Hong Xiuquan, had suffered deep personal disappointment. He had failed in the scholar examinations. In compensation, he had hallucinations of ascending into heaven and being told by the Christian God to exterminate demons. He came to believe that he was the younger son of Jesus. The demons came to be associated with the Manchu regime in Beijing and he and his southern associates spread their message further north to the Yangtze valley, offering a mix of religious mysticism and political and social reform.

The great city of Nanjing was captured and renamed Heavenly Capital. Power was divided among various commanders, each taking the title of king. Hong took the title of Heavenly King, but the most militarily effective was Yang Xiuqing, the Eastern King, who claimed to speak as the Holy Ghost. Dissension

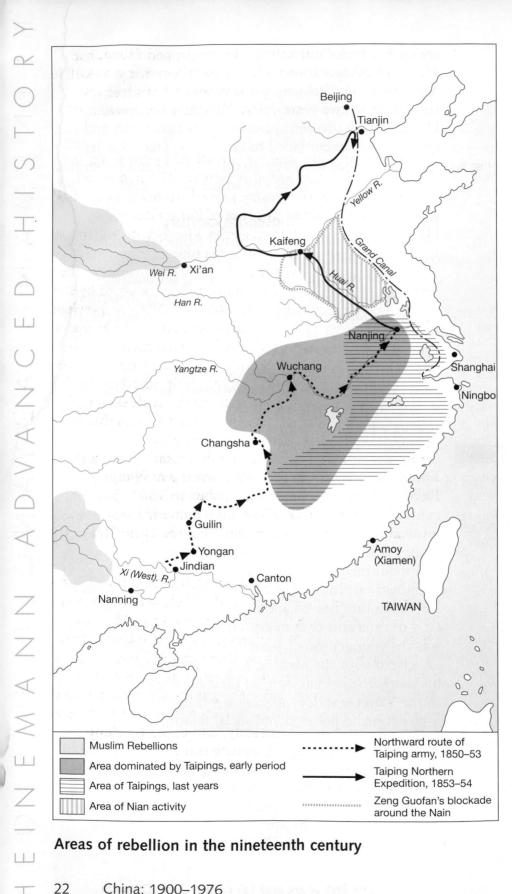

Areas of rebellion in the nineteenth century

inevitably broke out among the kings, and Hong, the Heavenly King, allied with the Northern King to kill Yang in 1856. The younger brother of Jesus had thus seen off the Holy Ghost. The Northern King was then also killed by Hong.

A complex array of forces was mustered by the Qing to regain control of the central provinces. The traditional **banner armies** of the regime proved strangely inept, but local gentry-led armies like that of Zeng Guofan from Hunan province and known as the Xiang Army (after the main river of Hunan) proved much more effective in fighting the fanatics. On leave in 1852, mourning in the correct form for his deceased mother, he was urged by the court to attempt to defeat the Taipings. With no previous military experience, he read up on military strategy and then formed an army, which proved much more effective than the Manchu banner armies. He came to embody the ideal Confucian scholar-official. Similarly, another force led by a British officer, Charles Gordon, made such a considerable impact on the Taiping power bases that it became known as the 'Ever Victorious Army'. A combination of various forces finally crushed the rising, but 100,000 rebels died in the storming of Nanjing. Hong and his rebellion both perished in 1864. But the continuing need for locally organised and led armies was ominous for the continuing control of the Qing Dynasty in Beijing.

A less destructive but still persistent rebellion broke out in the north along the course of the Yellow River. It was known as the Nian Rebellion and lasted from 1852 to 1868. Nian means band or group. The disruption caused by the flooding of the Yellow River in 1853 encouraged a bandit guerrilla movement to develop. It was a case of Robin Hood on a vast scale. The gentry and wealthy were pillaged and plundered (the bandits operated over an area the size of England). Eventually, armies led by **Zeng Guofan** and **Li Hongzhang**, who had played a major part in crushing the Taiping Rising, brought order to the devastated provinces.

KEY TERM

Banner armies were the traditional military organisation of the Manchu, dating back to the seventeenth century. Fighting tribesmen and their families were divided into eight banners – plain yellow, white, blue and red and the same colours with borders. Later, Chinese banner troops were added. By the nineteenth century, the system had ceased to produce efficient troops and they proved incapable of dealing with either the 'foreign devils' or rebellions.

KEY PEOPLE

Zeng Guofan (1811–72) and Li Hongzhang (1823–1901) were both jinshi holders and while promoting reform developed powerful regional bases which attracted envy and suspicion. Both were men of considerable ability and courage and made possible the prolongation of the Qing Dynasty, but both were very much from within the system. Zeng Guofan, in particular, exemplified the strengths and weaknesses of the Confucian scholar elite.

Reformers and their opponents

The challenges of the nineteenth century inevitably produced a questioning of China as it was. There were those alienated individuals like Hong Xiuquan, leader of the Taiping Rising, who wished to overthrow the regime and rebuild a new Jerusalem. There were those thoroughly westernised by travel abroad, like Sun Yat-sen, who wanted to modernise China and set up a republic, modelled on the USA. Most reformers, however, were not from the fringes of Chinese society like the above, but intelligent and reflective scholars and Manchu grandees who could see that things could not go on as they had been allowed to do. The price of survival was change.

The first such movement became known as the 'self-strengthening movement' and it grew in influence following the humiliations of the Arrow War and the defeat of the Taiping Rising. Its central figures were the Manchu Prince of the Blood, Prince Gong, who headed the new Zongli yamen, or foreign office, and was closely advised by Wenxiang, a jinshi scholar, who was its organising member. These two operated in Beijing, promoting education and modernisation. However, Prince Gong fell from favour and power in 1884 having crossed the powerful Empress Dowager, when he had one of her favourite court eunuchs executed.

In the provinces, two other Jinshi scholars played a major part in trying to push a reform agenda – Zeng Guofan and Li Hongzhang. The latter was governor general of Zhili and promoted both a modern navy and army and industrialisation, particularly railroads and telegraph communication. The movement produced individual triumphs like the Chinese Merchants Steam Navigation company in 1872 and the new foreign language school in 1862, but despite some success its limitations were cruelly exposed by the defeat of China by Japan in 1894.

The coup of 1898 and Han Discontent

As indicated already, the defeat of China in Korea by Japan gave massive impetus to the idea of reform among the scholar-gentry, who were to find leaders in two

KEY PEOPLE

Kang Youwei (1858–1927) was a constitutional monarchist and eminent thinker who really did wish to transform the Chinese state. As well as contributing to practical political reform, Kang challenged the whole Confucian intellectual tradition from the inside. He portrayed Confucius as a reformer, through the textual criticism of many revered Confucian texts. In 1898, he published *Confucius as a Reformer*, which had enormous intellectual impact. For the first time he gave China the idea of progress, a key western idea since the enlightenment but one alien to China, which thought in terms of endless repeated cycles since a mythical golden age.

KEY PEOPLE

The **Empress Dowager Cixi (1835–1908)** was the dominant person at the Qing court. She became regent for her son, who was a minor, in 1861 until 1873 and on his death in 1874 once again for her nephew until 1889. Even after this she continued to make the key decisions and, in 1898, organised a coup against her nephew the Emperor which left him powerless under house, or more accurately, palace arrest.

eminent Confucian scholars, **Kang Youwei** and his disciple, Liang Qichao. Both began to campaign for radical political changes involving the abolition of the traditional examination system and, even more radically, the notion of some degree of direct popular participation in politics through study groups and associations. The whole Chinese tradition was one of authoritarian top-down politics. All private societies were illegal. Study societies sprang up in Beijing and Shanghai and then Hunan province. Membership was drawn from the local gentry elites and teachers. The first newspapers appeared, published by the Study Societies and were often given away free. The Manchu authorities tried to close down both groups and papers and sometimes succeeded but in 1898 the unexpected happened.

Kang and his proposals reached the ear of the 27-year-old Guangxu emperor, through the influence of the imperial tutor. Kang presented extensive proposals for reform and was admitted to the inner cabinet of government. The result was the Hundred Days of Reform which lasted from mid-June to the third week in September (1898). Reform edicts poured from Beijing in the name of the Emperor. It looked as if China was going to embrace an even more radical course of reform than Japan had done in 1867. It was not to be. The **Empress Dowager Cixi**, who still wielded much power among the court officials and eunuchs of the forbidden city, rallied the conservative forces in Beijing and the provinces and launched a palace coup on 21st September. Kang and Liang escaped, but six leading reformers were put to death including Kang's brother. The Emperor was placed under close arrest and kept a prisoner for the rest of his life.

The coup of 1898 slowed the process of reform but did not stifle the demand for it, which continued to grow. Constitutionalists looked to the exiled Kang for leadership and the more radical to Sun Yat-sen and his more openly republican movement. In July 1905, Sun Yat-sen had founded the Tongmenghui or Revolutionary Alliance in Tokyo. It published a revolutionary paper which was smuggled around China and read by students and reformers. Underground cells sprang up in many of the major cities, plotting the downfall of the Qing. Seven abortive uprisings took place between 1906 and 1908 and the active membership had grown to about 10,000 by 1911. It was heavily supported and funded by overseas Chinese communities, particularly those of South East Asia.

The Japanese victory over Russia in 1905 was a powerful boost to the case for reform. Changes had been underway for some time in northern China in organising a modern army, well equipped and trained. The originator was Li Hongzhang. Under him was Yuan Shikai who eventually became the key military personality in China. He played a vital part in the events of 1911–12. Now, in 1905, a more modern army was accepted. The degree system was swept away in that year ending a thousand-year tradition. The first western style universities were introduced. Constitutional reforms were announced in 1906, but then

Centres of revolt, 1906–8

there was to be a nine year preparatory period, which produced widespread protests.

In October 1909, provincial assemblies were introduced which promptly became the focus of the simmering discontent. By this time, the central control of the provinces was slipping. The Empress Dowager died in 1908. For all her faults, she at least provided some semblance of authority and power. The day before she died, so did the Guangxu Emperor, probably murdered on her orders. Another minor, aged 3, now ascended the throne. The pace of reform accelerated, but it was too little too late. A national consultative council was established in 1910, and in 1911, what was meant to be a responsible cabinet. Unfortunately, nine of the 13 places went to imperial relatives and Manchu nobles. This excited Han resentment still further. Rebellious students began to cut off their pigtails, symbols of Han servitude to the ruling Manchu. Manchu troops sometimes executed such young men as insolent rebels.

The revolution of 1911–12

The final downfall was the product of a complex interplay of causes. The child Emperor who could not govern symbolised the impotence of the dynasty, yet it still took much to topple the monarchy. A massive budget deficit was developing to pay for reforms and the reparations dating back to the Boxer Rising. The new armies being phased in to replace the traditional banner armies were particularly expensive and many officers were infected with radicalism. Increased taxes were necessary and new duties were levied on tea, wine, salt and other products, as well as increased land taxes. As if to emphasise the loss of the Mandate of Heaven, torrential rains in 1910 and 1911 deluged the Yangtze valley, causing widespread floods. Grain prices rose, vast numbers died and the cities filled with homeless peasants.

It was agitation connected to the building of railways that actually triggered the revolt in some areas. The first years of the twentieth century witnessed a massive increase in railway construction, most of it under foreign direction and control. This produced a nationalist backlash and the founding of railway protection movements in many of China's provinces. Local associations of Chinese gentry and merchants attempted to raise money to take over and develop their local railways. Money was raised from overseas Chinese businessmen and the whole issue became a passionate symbol of the new Han Chinese national identity. In Beijing, things were seen differently. The provincial groups threatened central control and seemed slow and inefficient at getting on with railway building. Trunk railways were also profitable and might, if owned by the state, have made some impact on the mounting budget deficit. The upshot was a decision by a new minister of communications to nationalise all trunk lines with limited compensation. The decree was published in May. Money would be raised from foreign loans to continue building lines. To most Han Nationalists, here was a conspiracy of the Manchu oppressors and foreign devils, the twin curses of the last century. Riots and demonstrations spread. The whole of Sichuan province in the west was in chaos by the middle of September. The young Emperor issued a plaintive appeal on the orders of his guardians:

> *The whole Empire is seething. The minds of the people are perturbed ... All these things are my fault ....Being a very small person standing at the head of my subjects, I see that my heritage is nearly falling to the ground.*

On 9th October 1911, in the city of Hankou, an unfinished bomb being prepared by a group of young revolutionaries prematurely exploded. This triggered the **Wuchang Uprising**. Loyal troops had already been moved west to Sichuan. The Manchu governor of the city felt he had the situation under control when he arrested and executed on 10th October several members of the revolutionary group. Han troops still left in the neighbouring city of Wuchang mutinied, believing rumours that Han people were to be butchered. They wiped out the remaining Manchu regiment and then turned on any Manchu civilians they could find. Two months of confused fighting followed.

Many units of the new armies mutinied and there were widespread massacres of Manchu troops and civilians, particularly in the Shaanxi capital of Xi'an. Peasants and

KEY EVENT

The **Wuchang Uprising (1911)** is usually taken to mark the beginning of the revolution, as it was the first major city the Manchu authorities lost control of. Wuchang is one of three neighbouring cities on the Yangtze that are known by the joint name of Wuhan. The other two are Hankou and Hanyang.

others were forcibly deprived of their pigtails, to mark Han freedom. In other areas, loyal troops massacred rebels, often taking as a definition of rebel those without a pigtail.

In desperation, the court turned to the creator of the new armies, Yuan Shikai, and in November appointed him chief minister. In December, the Qing suffered a major blow when they lost control of Nanjing. Province after province now declared their independence from Qing rule – Sichuan on 22nd November and Shandong near to the capital on 12th December.

CONCLUSION

Sun Yat-sen had been in the USA at the time of the Wuchang Rising and now hastened back. He arrived in Shanghai on 25th December, and at the end of the month delegates from 16 provinces meeting in Nanjing elected him President of the Chinese Republic, but real power lay with the new armies and here Yuan Shikai was the key figure. Sun Yat-sen recognised the situation and wrote to him to say it was Yuan who should accept the presidency. The only Manchu strong man who could perhaps have rallied a last-ditch defence, the deputy chief of staff, was removed by a bomb in January. The Emperor's mother negotiated a favourable **abdication settlement** with Yuan Shikai who received an edict bestowing full powers from the Emperor on the same day as he announced his abdication. The blessings of the Emperor and the popular revolutionary leader thus confirmed the position of Yuan Shikai who had twice failed his juren examination. For the next few years the ruling of China would belong to soldiers not scholars.

SUMMARY QUESTIONS

1   In what ways does the growth of nationalism explain the downfall of Imperial China in 1911–12?

2   'It was China's humiliation at the hands of the west and Japan that destroyed the Qing regime.' How far do you agree with this statement?

KEY TERM

The **abdication settlement** gave the Emperor the right to continue to live in the Forbidden City and ownership of all the imperial treasures. He was given an income of US$4 million a year.

3   Why did attempts at reform fail to preserve the
    Imperial regime?

4   'A chapter of unfortunate accidents account for the
    revolution of 1911–12.' How far do you agree with
    this statement?

CHAPTER 3

The new China: a troubled and chaotic childhood, 1912–27

INTRODUCTION

The fall of a dynasty had sometimes been followed by a period of disintegration when the Chinese state seemed to fall apart. But a common heritage, whose living embodiment were the scholar-officials, kept the idea of unity alive until some soldier could re-impose political order and found a new dynasty. Now the Confucian examination system had been abolished, would China really fragment, like Europe at the end of the Roman Empire into separate kingdoms and republics? In reality, the disintegration was to be short lived, a mere 37 years. These years were, however, to be years of terror and misery for many ordinary Chinese men and women. The excitement and pig-tail cutting of 1911 led for many not to a fuller life but to rape, torture and death.

China in 1912 – Provinces

The new China: a troubled and chaotic childhood, 1912–27　　31

These years,1912–27, were marked by four important developments. Firstly, the attempt of one imperial general to seize the vacant throne. He failed but succeeded in stifling the first attempt in China to achieve representative government. Secondly, a period of chaos followed his death as various generals struggled for power and carved China up into sub-kingdoms. Thirdly, the Nationalist Party (GMD) re-emerged as a force to unite China and, fourthly, a tiny party, the Chinese Communist Party (CCP) was born and then rapidly grew to be first an ally and then a rival to the GMD.

THE YOUNG MAO ZEDONG

The young man who was to become emperor in all but name and found a new dynasty was just 18 when the last Qing Emperor abdicated. Like the founder of the long-lived Han Dynasty, he was a Han peasant. When Wuchang had exploded in revolt on 10th October 1911 (known as 10-10), the young **Mao Zedong** was in Changsha, the capital of Hunan province, and two days upstream from Wuchang. Earlier in the year in April, shortly after arriving in the provincial capital, he had seen his first newspaper, telling of a revolt in south China. He wrote a poster supporting it and cut off his pigtail. He had always been rebellious against his father. Now rebellion against the Manchu excited him. If the rebellion of April failed, that of 10-10 did not.

On Friday 13th October, the first news of the rising in Wuchang reached Changsha by steamer. The Changsha garrison mutinied and with little fighting, the city declared for the revolution. A few Manchu loyalists were beheaded and their heads left in the street near the governor's mansion. Like many of his fellow students Mao decided to join the revolutionary army, and there was talk of his unit marching north in support of Sun Yat-sen against Yuan Shikai. Sun Yat-sen conceded the presidency to Yuan Shikai (see Chapter 2, page 29) and the revolutionary forces were demobilised. Mao retired to his life as a student but an excited student, determined to play a part in the New China that was fizzing with ideas.

(see Chapter 2, page 29)

KEY PERSON

Mao Zedong (1893–1976) was the son of a peasant in Hunan province. His father had worked hard and become relatively wealthy as a grain dealer. Mao Zedong was the eldest son. He was wilful and rebellious, determined to be a scholar and teacher, not a financial scribe for his father's business. He rejected his family's choice of a bride and generally behaved in a very uncharacteristic way for a son of a traditional Confucian home. He was very attached to his mother. By sheer determination and wilfulness he got his way and was sent to secondary school in Changsha.

CHINA'S 'NEW YOUTH'

In the minds of clever young Chinese students like Mao Zedong, a mixture of European ideas fermented, but within a container structured by two thousand years of Chinese thought. Theories of evolution and change inspired by Darwin had an impact. The strong survived; the weak died and were eaten. Wasn't this what had happened to China in the nineteenth century? Mao's first published essay in April 1917 in the journal *New Youth* was concerned with PE – 'A study of physical education'. In it, he challenged established Chinese habits and his countrymen's preference for torpor over exertion. The New Youth came to embody the hopes of transforming Chinese society and culture. It was founded by **Chen Duxiu** in 1915 in Shanghai. To Chen Duxiu, the real enemy of change was Confucius; 'Down with Confucius' became his war cry. He urged students to show independence from parents and in particular to reject arranged marriages. The magazine was a publishing success among the young and educated and, from 1917, it adopted vernacular Chinese, not the complex classical language of the scholars. This was a written version of the northern dialect spoken across much of northern China. This vernacular or baihua involved far fewer characters and was simpler and easier to understand. In adopting baihua, the New Youth was striking a blow against the past, every bit as important as the abolition of the exam system in 1905.

KEY PERSON

Chen Duxiu (1879–1942) was born in the same year as Stalin. He held the first level of degree under the old system of exams. He studied abroad and became a champion of the new culture. He was Dean of the College of Letters in Beijing (1917–19) and a crucial figure in the founding of the Chinese Communist Party in 1921. From then until 1927, he was secretary-general and in effect its leader.

'We should die fighting'

The position of girls and women was central to any real cultural change. The feet of would-be modern young women were unbound, a process apparently causing nearly as much pain as the original binding. There were celebrated cases of female rebellion against the tyranny of the past and the power of the mother-in-law over the bride. A young woman in Gansu province, far from Beijing and Shanghai, threw herself down a well in opposition to a mother-in-law who forbade her to unbind her feet. In Mao's own Hunan there was the celebrated suicide of Miss Zhou who slit her own throat inside the canopied bridal chair rather than go through with an arranged marriage to a young man of the Wu Family.

Mao wrote a newspaper article on it in Changsha in November 1919. He condemned the social system which led to the suicide but objected to suicide as an answer – 'We should die fighting,' he wrote.

The whole cultural ferment came to be symbolised by events of 4th May 1919. News had arrived from Paris where the Versailles Peace Conference was taking place that the western powers, despite much talk of self-determination, freedom and a new world, were going to allow Japan to keep the German possessions in Shandong province. The result was an explosive protest from the students of Beijing university. On Sunday 4th May, 3,000 students from 13 different colleges assembled in Tiananmen Square, then a walled park. They protested at the latest humiliation of China and demanded their government assert itself against the Japanese. Their banners were written in the new clean-cut characters of the vernacular. Failing to get into the guarded foreign legation, they contented themselves with wrecking the house of the government minister closely associated with the treaty. It was not the event itself that mattered but what it came to represent: protest by youth against the past and China's humiliation.

A city-wide student union was established devoted to change – the **May 4th movement**. This was replicated across China in the great cities such as Shanghai, Wuhan and Tianjin. A general strike was held in Shanghai and the spreading tide of protest prevented the Chinese delegation from accepting the terms of the treaty. China refused to sign. In this sense, protest had worked.

The bigger question was how could and would China reinvent itself. Should the emphasis be on cultural change, destroying the legacy of Confucian thought in the minds of the Chinese people, or should the priority be ending national humiliation at the hands of foreign devils? What new political structures were appropriate for these tasks? The May 4th generation were concerned with all three and produced lots of different answers. Whose answer would predominate depended on the realities of political power, and since 1912 the exercise of political power was increasingly chaotic.

The May 4th movement was the name given to an explosion of yearning for change and national rebirth, articulated by students during the early 1920s. Some historians have seen it as the decisive event in setting the direction of China in the twentieth Century. Such a view is embodied in the recent study of twentieth-century China – Rana Mitter's *A Bitter Revolution* (2004).

THE RULE OF YUAN SHIKAI, 1912–16

The President of the new Chinese Republic, Yuan Shikai, was essentially a product of old Imperial China. His power base was the Beiyang Army which he had created in the first years of the twentieth century. It was the best fighting force in China and its divisional commanders were his protégées and they owed him loyalty. While he was there, these potential war lords could be kept in check. Sun Yat-sen's surrender of the presidency to him in 1912 was a simple recognition of this political reality. Power truly did come out of the muzzle of a rifle, but Sun Yat-sen and his supporters hoped that Yuan would rule as a constitutional president with a parliament modelled on the US Congress.

The assassin's bullet: a new dynasty

There was to be a senate elected by the different provincial assemblies and a house of representatives. Elections were held in December 1912. Four main parties emerged to contest the election and over 300 smaller local political groupings. The **National People's Party (GMD)** was created by Sun Yat-sen and his assistants out of the Revolutionary Alliance and it did remarkably well to win 43 per cent of the vote and 269 out of 596 seats in the house of representatives. The election appears as China's first exercise of democracy, even if the voting was restricted to male taxpayers, possibly 10 per cent of the population.

The GMD expected to form a government, and Sun Yat-sen delegated his most able assistant, the 30-year-old Song Jiaoren for the post of premier. Song Jiaoren went to Shanghai railway station on 20th March 1913 to board the train for Beijing and thus take power. An assassin's bullet ended his political career on the platform. It ended the hope that China might emerge as a constitutional democracy. Yuan Shikai was believed to be behind the assassination, and it soon became clear that his was a traditional solution to China's political problems. A new emperor and a new dynasty was called for. He knew just the man: himself.

In May, military governors sympathetic to the GMD were dismissed, and using his loyal Beiyang Army,

KEY TERM

The **Guomindang (GMD), the National People's Party,** is usually represented in the Wade–Giles system as Kuomintang (KMT). Its aims were to create a modern democratic China. The basic ideology was summed up in Sun Yat-sen's Three Prinicples of the People – nationalism, democracy and 'people's livelihood'. The last was rather vague and could be interpreted by the left of the party as equating with socialism.

Nanjing was occupied after heavy fighting with troops loyal to the GMD. The new assembly was forced by Yuan to elect him president for five years, the GMD MPs were expelled and the party declared illegal. Sun Yat-sen went into exile again. In all of this Yuan was acting with the sympathy and support of foreign powers (such as Britain), who above all wanted stability for trade and the security of their investments. They feared the anarchy that democracy might bring. Only the USA showed any real support and sympathy for the GMD. Britain held the greatest stake, with nearly 40 per cent of the total foreign investment in China in 1914. In October 1913, Britain formally recognised Yuan's regime and other powers followed suit.

The support of foreign powers

The recognition and support of the foreign powers was vital as the regime rested on foreign loans. Less and less money was reaching the central treasury in Beijing and most of the provincial land taxes were remaining in the hands of provincial military governors whose support Yuan needed.

Luckily, most of the foreign powers were to be distracted from taking further advantage of China by the outbreak of the First World War. Only Japan remained to take advantage of further weakness and, in January 1915, presented the **Twenty-one Demands**. Resisting some of the most humiliating demands, which would have destroyed Chinese sovereignty, Yuan was forced to accede on 7th May, which would be declared National Humiliation Day.

The concessions to Japan were a body blow to Yuan and his ambitions. Nevertheless, he pressed ahead. He performed the ancient rituals of ploughing and sacrifice at the Temple of Agriculture and the Altar of Heaven as emperors had done for hundreds of years. The date of his enthronement was announced. This simply served to trigger revolts. Yunnan in the south-west declared its independence and others followed suit. Yuan reluctantly back-peddled and dropped his plans in March 1916. In June, he died at 56 years of age a broken man. The first would-be emperor had failed, but he had destroyed the

KEY EVENT

The **Twenty-one Demands** were a group of economic and political demands which Japan presented in January of 1915 after seizing German concessions in Shandong province. Yuan agreed to the wide-ranging economic concessions but refused those last group of demands which, by installing Japanese advisers in various branches of Chinese government, would in effect have created a Japanese protectorate over China.

democratic experiment. Republican government as envisaged by Sun Yat-sen seemed to have little future. A restoration of the Emperor or at best an autocratic presidency seemed inevitable.

The Vice President, who had reluctantly taken the job, tried to reconvene the parliament of 1912 but, in 1917, fell victim to a coup by the most forceful of Yuan's commanders, the man who captured Nanjing for Yuan in 1913. Now in 1917, Zhang Xun seized Beijing and tried to restore Puyi. In July, he was forced out by rival generals and the era of the warlords had truly begun.

THE ERA OF THE WARLORDS, 1917–26

What now developed in China in the absence of any legitimate authority was something akin to the state of nature described by the great English seventeenth-century philosopher, Thomas Hobbes. In Hobbes' famous words, 'The life of man was nasty, brutish and short.' It was no better for women; in some ways it was worse.

The year 1917 witnessed the failed attempt to restore the Manchu Dynasty, referred to above, but also China's declaration of war on Germany. This, it was hoped, would bring a new self-respect to China as it joined the side of Britain, France, the USA and Japan in the First World War. At the very least, the German concessions in Shandong province would be returned to the control of Beijing. This again, as indicated above, was not to be. The victors, meeting at Versailles in 1919, awarded the German concessions to Japan not China and the news of this fresh humiliation triggered the 4th May demonstration and the subsequent movement of national renewal bearing its name. Outer Mongolia was also lost to even nominal control, and Japan and the new Soviet Union vied there for domination. It eventually emerged in 1924 as the People's Republic of Mongolia, closely tied to communist Russia. Internally, Chinese politics might have been likened to comic opera or farce were it not for the tragic consequences for ordinary Chinese citizens. Yuan Shikai's generals vied with one another for control of a particular region and for the ultimate prize, control of Beijing and the central government that in theory functioned there.

Warlords came in all shapes and sizes. Some, like the Christian General, were large. Converted to Methodism, he banned foot-binding, opium and brothels, and wore a simple almost shapeless uniform over his large frame. His troops were among the best trained and best disciplined and he had them sing a song about the need to conserve ammunition to the tune of 'Hark the Herald Angels Sing'.

If Feng represented the more acceptable side of 'warlordism', Zhang Zong chang, the 'Dogmeat General' of Shandong province, represented the converse. He was said to have the body of an elephant, the brain of a pig and the temperament of a tiger. He gave his numerous concubines numbers as there were too many to remember their names. He and his troops behaved with incredible brutality. They enjoyed 'opening melons' as they called splitting the skulls of anyone who crossed them. Severed heads were hung from telegraph poles to encourage subservience in the civil population.

In Shanxi province, near to the area dominated by the Christian General, was the rather stout Model Governor Yan Xishan, who introduced numerous reforms into his area, drawing on all manner of western ideas. Life in his province was perhaps more tolerable than in many others, but he organised an efficient secret police to head off any opposition. Wu Peifu, the Philosopher General, dominated Wuhan and the central Yangtze region. Devoted to Confucian thought and proud of his calligraphy, he also had a weakness for alcohol in the form of imported brandy. Not surprisingly, this was somewhat disapproved of by the Methodist Christian General who sent him gifts of water. In the large western province of Sichuan there were as many as 50 generals battling for supremacy at one time. Most

Chiang Kaishek (centre) and the warlords, Feng Yuxiang and Yan Xishan

powerful of all the warlords was Zhang Zuolin of Manchuria. Known as the Old Marshal, he was in origin a bandit. He governed an area north of the Great Wall as large as western Europe and wore the world's largest pearl on his black skull cap.

KEY EVENT

The **wars of 1920–26** were a series of struggles between different groups of generals allied into cliques, such as the so-called Zhili clique led by Wu Peifu, the Philosopher General. This often involved a struggle to control Beijing and the nominal central government. Foreign powers tended to favour particular generals. The Christian General was ironically backed by the USSR, the Old Marshal in Manchuria by Japan and Britain pinned her hopes on Wu Peifu. The most bloody of the conflicts was that between Wu Peifu and the Manchurians in 1924 and this weakened both, making the GMD's Northern Expedition of 1926 possible.

Whatever their personal characteristics, all needed money for their troops. In 1916, there were about half a million soldiers under Yuan. By the end of the bitter **wars of 1920–26**, the numbers had trebled. Most were ill-disciplined and untrained peasants, but they needed feeding and paying. Everything was taxed and cash squeezed from a suffering peasantry. Even the Christian General pilfered to feed his army. All printed money with little supporting precious metal. The result was inflation and depreciation of the currencies. Zhang Zuolin of Manchuria was aware of the problem but had little grasp of economics. He had great faith, however, in the gun. Merchants in his province were called in before him and told to ensure the currency's stability. Five were shot to emphasise the point.

If the warlords were the source of much of the suffering and upheaval, nature added to China's woes. There was a drought in northern China in 1918 and famines in 1920 and 1921. Flooding brought misery in 1923–25. The death toll from these ran into millions.

The end of the Qing had not brought improvement for most people. Yet there were positive signs in some areas. Industry began to grow rapidly in some cities especially in Shanghai and in southern Manchuria. The First World War had frozen the supply of goods from Europe and the shortages began to be made up from home-produced products. This was particularly true of textiles. Without the deadening hand of an all-powerful state and where the chaos of warlord violence and crime were not too destructive, private initiative and enterprise could flourish as never before. The seeds of China's industrial development had at least been planted. All that was needed was political stability and a state that would look favourably on private enterprise.

Two groups came together in the 1920s to try to provide unity and stability, but even before the decade was out they had become bitter enemies. Only one would rule a reinvigorated and reunited China. Both drew their inspiration and energy from the May 4th movement. Both owed much to Russian help and the Moscow based **Comintern**. One was the newly founded Communist Party. The other was the resurrected GMD.

THE BIRTH OF THE CHINESE COMMUNIST PARTY (CCP)

The new Soviet government in Russia aroused interest and hope among many young Chinese revolutionaries. It seemed that the Bolsheviks in Russia had done what they wanted to do in China. An old regime had been overthrown and, despite the intervention of the western powers in the Russian civil war, the Bolsheviks had triumphed in 1921. Furthermore, the new Russian government appealed to Chinese nationalism. It offered to surrender all concessions made to the old Imperial Russian government by the Qing and condemned all the special privileges held in the treaty ports by the western powers. In short, it seemed an obvious model and ally to those Chinese wishing to transform China.

Chen Duxui, the founder of New Youth and leading light in the May 4th movement, was increasingly interested in Marxism. In May 1919, he devoted a whole issue of New Youth to the subject. Small Marxist study groups were founded in Shanghai and Beijing. Mao Zedong, newly returned to Changsha in 1920, founded a group there. Total numbers were very small but the arrival of Comintern agents would transform this.

Initially, the key figure was Gregory Voitinski who made contact with Chen Duxui in May 1920. The first translation of the Communist Manifesto into Chinese was arranged and Chen Duxui was appointed secretary of a provisional central committee on the Russian model. The following year, a forceful new Comintern agent, a Dutchman named Hendricus Sneevliet, arrived in Shanghai in June and promptly organised a meeting, generally held to be the founding congress of the party in July 1921. It was held in secret in a classroom at a girls' school in the French concession of Shanghai. All the delegates were teachers or students. Mao Zedong was

KEY TERM

The **Comintern** or **Third Communist International** was established in Moscow in March 1919 by the new Bolshevik government, nominally by the First Congress. Its aim was to promote worldwide proletarian revolution, whose prospects were thought to be excellent at the time. The Second Congress in 1920 laid down rules for joining which stressed that any national communist party was a branch of an international army committed to the overthrow of capitalism.

summoned from Changsha as the representative of Hunan province to join 12 other delegates. The most important figure, Chen Duxui, was not there but was elected secretary-general in his absence. Hendricus Sneevliet, who opened the conference, pushed the official line of developing links with the proletariat. It was rightly pointed out by one delegate that the proletariat was not very large in China and most had never heard of Marxism. There was resistance to working with the GMD. The congress was forced to move venues because of a police raid, but the CCP was established and agreed to join the Comintern.

The influence of Russian advisers was paramount and, from the start, partially resented, but then the Comintern provided US$5,000 per annum to keep the fledgling party alive. Sneevliet had caused particular controversy at the founding meeting by urging cooperation with the GMD. This line was insisted upon by Moscow who saw the GMD as a more useful tool than the tiny new Communist Party. The issue was raised again and again at meetings. In the 1922 congress of the CCP it was agreed to seek a temporary alliance to combat warlords and in the third congress in 1923 it was agreed that communists could not only cooperate with the GMD but actually join the party as a 'bloc within'.

Mao followed the official line and in 1923 joined the GMD. His obedience to the official line won him membership of the central committee. For the next three years he worked closely within the United Front as a GMD official like many other good communists, but Mao did not ingratiate himself into the inner circle around Chen Duxui. He was not one of the party's great intellectuals. He also did not share their faith in the role of the tiny Chinese industrial proletariat. He was increasingly attracted by the ideas of Peng Pai, who laid emphasis on the revolutionary potential of the downtrodden Chinese peasant. In 1925, he was excluded from the central committee, falling victim to the power struggles that perpetually rent the party. He joined Peng Pai in a training institute for rural militants later that year and began to develop his theories of rural revolution which were to serve him and his party well.

Contrary to the expectation of its Russian patrons, the CCP had expanded rapidly from 200 members in 1922 to 7000 in early 1926 and 30,000 by the end of that year. The expansion in 1925 and after was particularly helped by the **May 30th incident**. Certainly, by 1927, when membership may have reached 58,000 and the CCP was the third largest in the world, it was a major force in China. As such, it was a cause of real concern to many within the GMD, despite their alliance.

The reorganisation triumph of the GMD

The new Bolshevik Russia was riding two horses in China and regarded the CCP as the lesser of the two. Sun Yat-sen, an established political figure, was seen as more worthy of support and patronage than a collection of Chinese intellectuals fascinated by Marxist theory. A senior Soviet diplomat, Adolf Joffe, was sent to make formal contact with Sun Yat-sen in January 1923. They agreed that national unity and independence were the prime aim and the USSR would sponsor the GMD in achieving this. Later in the year a more permanent Soviet representative arrived, **Mikhail Borodin**, who over the next three years would transform the GMD and China. Borodin sought to remodel the GMD into a party like Lenin's Bolshevik party, one enjoying mass support but with an all-powerful central committee; in other words, a party which could form the basis of a populist dictatorship. Sun Yat-sen's ideas were repackaged by Borodin and the Three Principles of the People (nationalism, democracy and 'people's livelihood') became the party's mantra. Sun Yat-sen was named party leader for life.

Borodin's influence was cemented by shiploads of arms into Canton, Sun Yat-sen's base. Sun Yat-sen was convinced that he needed his own army to deal with the warlords and break out of Canton where he lived a precarious existence before his deal with Joffe. Now with a powerful backer, the GMD gained a new lease of life. To give Sun Yat-sen's new party more power, more than arms were needed. An army different from the ragged, ill-disciplined levies of the warlords was desirable. The Soviet regime offered them money and advisers to support a new military academy. On an island close to

Canton, the Whampoa Military Academy was founded. Borodin approved the appointment of a young soldier, **Jiang Jieshi**, as commandant. He had impressed the Russians already, spending the latter part of 1923 in Moscow on a training course. A young intellectual communist newly returned from studying in France was appointed deputy political commissar at the college. His name was **Zhou Enlai**. The close cooperation of the young CCP and the reinvigorated GMD seemed to be working, oiled by Russian roubles.

In 1925, Sun Yat-sen, still only 59, was diagnosed with liver cancer and died that year. It was not clear who would succeed him as the totem figure of Chinese Nationalism. Chiang Kaishek made his bid in 1926 when he insisted that the GMD launch a strike for control of central China. The result was the **Northern Expedition,** which started out in July 1926. It was a joint triumph for Chiang's new army, the **NRA**, and communist propaganda among the peasantry.

The Northern Expedition

Chiang Kaishek relied heavily on his Russian military adviser, General Blyucher, known as Galen, but there was no doubt that his Whampoa Military Academy had produced an army superior to that of the warlords. Its troops were forbidden to prey on the peasants and were ordered to pay for any food. The peasants were subjected in advance to propaganda from the Farmers' Movement Training Institute in which Mao Zedong was a senior figure. Peasants served as guides and labourers for the NRA against their local warlords and by 10th October Wuhan on the Yangtze was captured from Wu Peifu, the Philosopher General. Galen had taught the Chinese the value of the indirect approach, circling around an enemy, and certainly the NRA fought well. The warlord's troops lacked their motivation and were often short of pay. Chiang proved himself an able diplomat, isolating first one warlord then another and striking deals, using extensive bribery.

From Wuhan, Chiang turned east and began his advance down the Yangtze to the great cities of Nanjing and

Shanghai, but already tension between Chiang and the CCP had reached breaking point.

THE END OF THE UNITED FRONT, 1927

Chiang had already shown his suspicion of the growing influence of the Communists and the Russian tutors of the GMD in 1925. Suspecting a communist coup in Canton in March of that year, he had suddenly arrested 30 Russian advisers. Borodin, under pressure from Moscow, still stressed the importance of the GMD rather than the Communists and agreed to rein in the Communists within the party and some sort of harmony was preserved. Mao loyally emphasised the need to continue cooperation and stressed, in his new role with the peasantry, the need for restraint in attacking landlords.

Increased political divisions within the GMD

When the Northern Expedition was launched in July 1926 and Chiang was sworn in as commander-in-chief of the expedition, the United Front appeared to be alive and well. The harmony was embodied in the mobilisation order for the expedition. Yet there were bitter tensions within the GMD. In August 1925, a leading advocate of cooperation with the Communists, Liao Zhongkai, had been assassinated. The problem basically arose from the conflict of interests between the nationalist gentry and merchants who provided the money for the GMD and the intellectual activists who were keen on mobilising the peasants and workers and thus cooperating with the communists.

In January 1926, the party showed a three-way split, with 16 per cent of the right-wing delegates looking to Hu Hanmin, a rather conservative associate of Sun Yat-sen; 23 per cent centrists who might be said to support Chiang; and 60 per cent leftists favouring close cooperation with the Communists. The most eminent of this group was **Wang Jingwei**.

The initial success of the northern expedition was a triumph for the United Front. Left-wing historians have stressed the importance of peasant activists in undermining the warlords' power from below. Nationalists have stressed the quality of the new army of the GMD. In reality, money was the key. Chiang appreciated that much of his success was due to bribery of rival generals. He was a hard-nosed realist as well as a nationalist. He realised the need to keep the gentry and merchant community on side and how important it was not to upset the foreign concessionary powers to the point where they intervened on the side of the warlords against the nationalists. As a member of the Chinese moneyed classes, although not of the elite, he was also frightened by the growing power of unions and peasant organisations. Personally, he was being subjected to a charm offensive by the powerful Soong family which was to have a considerable effect on Chiang's life.

Chiang had a series of clashes with the left of the GMD over strategy after the capture of Wuhan and he was particularly worried by the **attacks on western interests** in Hankou in January and later in Nanjing in March by leftist members of the GMD/Communist forces. He aimed to capture Shanghai from warlord Sun Zuanfang. There were 22,000 troops in Shanghai and 42 foreign warships. To alienate the foreigners would make his task impossible. Nevertheless, Shanghai was occupied by nationalist troops towards the end of March 1927, aided by a general strike and a left-wing insurrection organised by the Communists. However, by the second week in April, Chiang had made an arrangement with various groups to eliminate the Communists in Shanghai.

Massacre in Shanghai

After a series of meetings with representatives of the commercial classes and the Shanghai underworld, Chiang withdrew to Nanjing leaving his army under the control of the Communist-hating Guangxi general, Bai Chongxi. Early in the morning of 12th April, heavily armed members of **Big-eared Du's** Green Gang moved through the international settlement to attack the union strongholds in the working-class districts of the city. The most important union leader had been invited to Big-eared Du's for dinner and invited to change sides. He refused, was beaten into insensibility and then buried alive. In the course of the morning the left in Shanghai were brutally attacked. Du's men, aided by nationalist troops, beheaded or shot many. Some were thrown alive

---

into the fires of locomotives at the South Railway Station. The police put the official death toll for the day at 400. The left-wing American journalist, Edgar Snow, thought the figure somewhere between 5,000 and 10,000. Most today would think Snow more accurate than the police. The future communist Prime Minister Zhou Enlai escaped. It was said Chiang had ordered him to be allowed to escape to repay a favour Zhou Enlai had done for him in Canton.

CONCLUSION

The GMD left-wing in Wuhan maintained common cause with the Communists and on 17th April 1927 expelled Chiang from the Party. In Nanjing, Chiang formed a rival GMD government. He, however, had money. The deals he brokered with the powerful commercial interests in Shanghai gave him access to the funds he needed to maintain momentum. The left-wing GMD in Wuhan struggled to pay the troops that remained loyal to them. They resorted to printing money which rapidly became worthless.

Chiang played a clever game, using the Christian General, who negotiated with both the Wuhan GMD and Chiang's group in Nanjing. The Christian General finally came down on Chiang's side and most of the GMD broke with the Communists and made their peace with Chiang. His manoeuvrings were masterly if morally detestable. Perhaps his cruellest decision was to abandon his wife, known as Jenny, in order to marry into the powerful Soong family. He married the youngest Soong sister which made him a relative to the deceased Sun Yat-sen. To Chiang, any sacrifice was justified in the pursuit of his political goal.

By September 1927, Moscow finally accepted that the United Front with the GMD had ended. Borodin left in July and Chiang's former close Russian adviser, General Blyucher, alias Galen, left slightly later. Chiang insisted on seeing him off before he went and begged him to return. The Communists were left with little alternative to armed struggle. The leadership was committed to a rising of the proletariat. The result was the first solo communist military action, which took place in the city of Nanchang, the capital of Jiangxi. It is usually referred

The Nationalists repressed the uprising in Canton with great severity

to as the Autumn Harvest Uprising. It was rapidly crushed. On Stalin's orders a second rising took place in Canton in December. Thousands died in its repression. The government in Moscow had been taken completely by surprise by the events of 1927. Stalin had backed the United Front enthusiastically and denounced those Chinese Communists who wanted to go it alone as Trotskyite. The initial response to the Shanghai coup was one of smug self-congratulation, that all this had been foreseen and Chiang had merely revealed himself as the reactionary he always was but that cooperation should continue with the left GMD. As this option disintegrated, Moscow not for the first time, did a complete somersault and now adopted the policy previously denounced as unrealistic. Mao Zedong who had already struck out on his own with his commitment to peasant insurrection was well placed to benefit from the events of 1927 if he could avoid being killed.

SUMMARY QUESTIONS

1 Why did the control of the government in Beijing over the provinces of China break down in the years 1912–26?

2 What explains the success of the Northern Expedition of 1926?

3 In what ways did the USSR influence political developments in China in the period 1921–27?

4 Why did the United Front come to an end in 1927?

CHAPTER 4

Rival visions of the new China, 1928–37

INTRODUCTION

In 1927, the United Front of the Nationalist Party (GMD) and the Chinese Communist Party (CCP) had ended with a series of bloodbaths. Chiang Kaishek had broken free of Russian control and weakened the left wing of the GMD. He hoped that this would leave him the sole standard bearer of Sun Yat-sen's party and the sole inheritor of Sun Yat-sen's legacy. He would be the man, he hoped, to reunite China. He had certainly weakened the Communists, particularly in the cities, but he had not destroyed them. From their new rural guerrilla bases, they offered a different and peasant-orientated vision of a new China. Chiang's vision was rooted in the cities.

THE UNIFICATION OF CHINA, 1928

Chiang's consolidation of power

Stalin denounced Chiang as the reactionary tool of Shanghai capitalism. This relationship was not obvious to Shanghai capitalists. Chiang was obsessed with his dream of unification and for this he needed money to pay his army and continue the progress of the Northern Expedition to Beijing. Money was in short supply and the Shanghai business community was the one to produce it. The president of the chamber of commerce was asked for a large loan. He refused, and his property was promptly confiscated. Rich merchants were squeezed in every way possible, including extortion, and even had to ransom their kidnapped children. In many ways, Chiang's approach had much in common with that of the fascist parties of Europe. He had little respect for private enterprise and capitalism *per se* but, like Hitler, he saw it as a more efficient system for generating money and thereby serving as a milch-cow for his military/nationalist dreams. By such ruthless methods and more effectively in the long term by appointing his new brother-in-law,

KEY PEOPLE

T V Soong (1894–1971)
was the eldest brother of
Chiang Kaishek's new
wife. Like his father he was
a successful businessman
and, at one stage, reputedly
the richest man in the
world. Chiang made him
finance minister in 1928.
Soong raised the money for
Chiang's unification drive and
various campaigns against
the Communists, but he
quarrelled with Chiang in
1933 over escalating military
expenditure and was replaced
by the husband of his elder
sister, H H Kung. The job
was thus kept in the family.
Soong then became head of
the Bank of China. He later
served as Ambassador to
Washington and from 1944
as Prime Minister.

**Zhang Xueliang (1898–
2001)** was always known
as the Young Marshal to
distinguish him from his
father, the Old Marshal. He
had a reputation as a playboy
with a taste for drink, drugs,
golf and ballroom dancing.
He appeared to the Japanese
officers of the Kwantung
Army to be perfect as a
malleable puppet. They were
wrong. He arranged the
murder of his father's chief
of staff who was in the pay
of the Japanese and brought
Manchuria into the new
GMD China in return for
dominance in the north.

T V Soong as Finance Minister, he was able to gather a
war chest for the resumption of the conquest of the north.

His allies were Feng, the Christian General of Henan and
the north west, and Yan Xishan, the Model Governor of
Shanxi. The major opponent was the most powerful of the
warlords, Zhang Zuolin of Manchuria. Chiang advanced
north clashing in May with Japanese forces at Jinan in
Shandong. It was a bitter foretaste of what was to come.
There was a short but bloody period of fighting between
Chiang's forces and the Japanese garrison. Both sides
committed atrocities including the blinding and
castration of surrendered prisoners. Chiang eventually
side-stepped the Japanese to move on north to Beijing,
with Feng attacking from the west. Zhang withdrew
north into Manchuria but was killed in a bomb incident
organised by officers of the Japanese Kwantung Army of
Korea and Manchuria who were already partially out of
control. They had hoped that his son, **Zhang Xueliang**,
would be a more subservient puppet. They were
disappointed, and in December he accepted the authority
Chiang and the GMD government in Nanjing had given
him. Chiang's dream looked to be almost fulfilled. From
Canton in the south to Mukden in Manchuria, there was
now one Chinese government. All were part of the new
nationalist China. Only Tibet and the extreme west of the
Qing Empire remained independent.

Chiang's China

The new China had a flag of a white sun on blue and red.
In the grandiose mausoleum of Sun Yat-sen, a national
shrine was created just outside Nanjing, the new capital.
Sun's body was transferred from Beijing in an elaborate
ceremony supervised by Chiang. Beijing meaning
northern capital was renamed Beiping and abandoned as a
capital. Chiang preferred to be in his heartlands, close to
the cash he needed. Chiang's power rested primarily on
his control of the army. Rather like Yuan Shikai before
him, it was the links forged with a burgeoning officer
corps that gave him his hold. His time as commandant of
the Whampoa Military Academy in the early 1920s had
enabled him to create an influential network of supporters
who looked to him for patronage and protection. His
marriage into the Soong family gave him vital links to

the richest sectors of Chinese commerce and banking and helped him cultivate the position of Sun Yat-sen's heir.

The key positions he held were chairman of the military committee and commander in chief, chairman of the executive Yuan (governmental executive committee, i.e. prime minister) and head of the party. At one point, he held 25 different positions simultaneously, He displayed a single-minded ruthlessness and capacity for hard work which impressed, but he found it hard to delegate and was appalled at the slipshod methods and attitudes to work common among Chinese civil servants. His answer was a punishing workload for himself and long lectures to his subordinates delivered in a high-pitched voice. He also had a genius for manipulation and compromise with erstwhile enemies and enjoyed playing off one group against another. As in Nazi Germany, duplicate or triplicate organisations were created, seeking to do the same job and entering into rivalry. Chiang remained the necessary man in the middle.

The army was the bedrock of the regime and its officer corps the new mandarins. A career in the army was probably the quickest way to power and wealth. On the other hand, it did involve fighting. There was hardly a time in the 20 years after unification when it was not engaged in military activity, against troublesome warlords, the Communists and the Japanese. A former Whampoa cadet, Dai Li, headed the much feared **Military Bureau of Statistics**. This was the secret police. It ran a huge network of spies, organised assassinations and was in short prepared to do anything to defend Chiang and his regime.

The power base of the GMD

The main social underpinning for the regime came from two groups, the commercial elite of the cities and the gentry and richer peasants in the countryside. Most of the GMD elite came from the urban middle and upper classes, symbolised by the Soong family. These formed a tiny proportion of the population. During the 1930s, only 4.5 per cent of the population lived in cities of over 100,000. While many of this urban elite benefited from the GMD regime and certainly preferred it to the

The **Military Bureau of Statistics** was in effect the secret police organisation of the GMD. It was clearly outside any legal restraints and regularly used torture and murder. Its network of spies added to the paranoia in the communist camp, which responded with similar and even more misplaced brutality, i.e. the GMD tended to target known opponents and communist suspects, but the Communists often tortured and killed loyal Communists fearing them as infiltrators.

communist alternative, the GMD was not an ideal patron of capitalism. The legal security for property and the rule of law, which existed in Britain and North America, did not exist under Chiang. Constant government interference wedded to rampant corruption impeded the development of a really prosperous capitalist society and alienated many who were initially attracted to the GMD regime as a new broom offering honesty and a renewed sense of national pride.

The rural elite were also, ultimately something of a handicap. They attracted the increasing resentment of the deprived peasant masses, who lived on a knife edge with tiny holdings of land. Floods and drought could at any time bring them starvation and death, and envious eyes were cast on the larger land holdings of the gentry. Their hold on the village communities was weakening. Land was increasingly bought up by absentee army officers or bureaucrats whose only interest in the village was how much rent could be extracted. Traditional village life with its orderly Confucian hierarchy was collapsing and the regime for all its talk of revolution and a new China could not really bid for the peasants' support without upsetting its own bedrock officer class.

The Regime tried to boost support for itself by creating a new unifying ideology known as the **New Life Movement**. In many ways, it represented a return to Confucian values and Old Life Movement might have been a more accurate name. This appeared partially inspired by Mussolini's fascist doctrines, as was an organisation known as the **Blueshirts**. Chiang appears to have been much taken with Mussolini's regime, whose answers to Italy's problems, Chiang felt, were relevant to the situation in newly unified China.

Chiang's GMD government did have some real successes, and revisionist studies such as that edited by F Wakeman and R L Edmunds (*Reappraising Republican China*, 2000) make a point of these rather than the plethora of problems that traditionalist studies have emphasised. Three thousand miles of new railway were constructed and the long-projected link between Wuhan and Canton completed, making it possible to travel by rail from Beiping in the north to Canton in the south. Steamer

KEY TERMS

The **New Life Movement** was promoted from 1934 onwards as an answer to Communism. It was a mixture of traditional Confucian values of respect for parents and authority with the hopes of Sun Yat-sen for national renewal and an element of Christian missionary social reformism. Chiang had high hopes, but it descended into trivia like the campaigns against urinating, spitting and smoking in public and careful regulation of women's clothing.

The **Blueshirts** were headed by Whampoa cadets, of whom the most important was Dai Li. It was intended to set an example of selfless and ascetic dedication to national service, its members promising to give up whoring, gambling and drunkenness. In practice, its most important work was assisting Dai Li's other organisation in assassinating opponents of the regime.

transport expanded on the rivers and along the coast. The first airlines started up and 15,000 miles of road had been built by 1936. In the great cities like Shanghai there were the beginnings of a consumer society with cinemas and shopping malls and, most importantly, electric power. Politically, Chiang could point not only to the formal reunification of China but the reduction of the number of **foreign concessions** from 33 to 13 achieved through negotiation. China regained full control of its own tariffs and custom collection service in 1928 and, as a result, revenues from customs trebled by 1931. Parts of the army were much improved with the aid of German instructors and a new unified currency was introduced in 1935.

In 1931, a provisional constitution was issued, which with its examination and control bureaux, showed a tendency to return to the old imperial model for the civil service. Although there were to be separate executive, legislative and judicial bodies, Chiang's China was a one-party state very much under his personal dictatorship.

However, for all the achievements, Chiang's China remained a third-world country of appalling poverty and problems. If the number of secondary schools trebled between 1926 and 1935, there were still only 3,000, serving half a million out of a population of 500 million. If railroad construction had improved, there was still less railway track than in the state of Illinois in the USA. If government revenue had improved, it was still totally inadequate and heavily dependent on tariffs. The old imperial land tax could not be collected and was left to the provinces. Every year the government faced a deficit to be funded by borrowing or more illegal methods. The constant need to engage in military activities hindered and reduced spending on health and education. The old warlords were fickle allies. The Guangxi Clique from west of Canton, who had been Chiang's longest serving partners, rebelled in 1929 and had to be bribed and intimidated into submission. The Christian General proved troublesome by showing considerable independence in 1930, and the extreme western provinces were never under the effective control of the Nanjing government. Most worrying of all to Chiang were the Communists and the Japanese. The Japanese were a

Foreign concessions were areas of foreign jurisdiction within Chinese cities. They had been created and added to by the various treaties forced on China by foreign powers, since 1842. The concessions arose from the assertion of the foreign powers that Chinese courts were unfair and a foreigner accused of a crime would be tried in a court controlled by a consul from his own country. Foreigners often claimed the extension of this right to their Chinese employees. It came to represent a real infringement of Chinese sovereignty and a constant reminder of national humiliation.

disease of the skin, he claimed, but the Communists were a disease of the heart.

THE COMMUNIST PARTY SURVIVES AND CHANGES ITS STRATEGY

In a very short time, several hundred million peasants in China's central, southern and northern provinces will rise like a fierce wind or tempest, a force so swift and violent that no power, however great, will be able to suppress it.

So wrote Mao Zedong in the February of 1927. He had announced to the party leadership his conversion to a new approach to the achievement of revolution and gaining power. It arose from a month-long journey he had undertaken in his native Hunan studying the peasant question. It was, of course, heresy to the traditional Marxist intellectuals who dominated the party and believed the urban proletariat should lead the revolution following the Russian model.

The massacre of the revolutionary proletariat in Shanghai in April 1927 and the later crushing of the rising in Canton opened the way for the triumph of Mao's approach as the only way for the party to survive and prosper. Its future would lie in the countryside not the towns. The ending of the United Front with the GMD also removed the restraints on the party's rural agitators who hitherto had tried to moderate their peasant attacks on those gentry who backed the GMD. Moscow gave the new line its blessing, which would eventually help Mao's ascent, but Mao also clashed with senior figures in the party over the need to organise a revolutionary army as opposed to simply relying on the insurrection of the masses. He raised a force composed of peasants and bandits in Hunan and launched attacks in the autumn as directed by the party. These were known as the Autumn Harvest Uprisings The attacks failed and the party chiefs in hiding in Shanghai blamed Mao for opportunism and bandit tendencies. Mao's chief critic was the head of the party's military committee, **Zhou Enlai**.

The party was in fact in serious trouble. Party membership had been 57,000 in May 1927, but by December it was 10,000. Thousands of members and

KEY PERSON

Zhou Enlai (1898–1976) joined Chiang's Whampoa Military Academy in 1924 as a deputy political director during the period of the United Front. He escaped from Shanghai in 1927 and was a member of the Central Committee from that year until 1976. Suave, highly intelligent and a brilliant negotiator, it was not until the late 1930s that he firmly and finally attached himself to Mao.

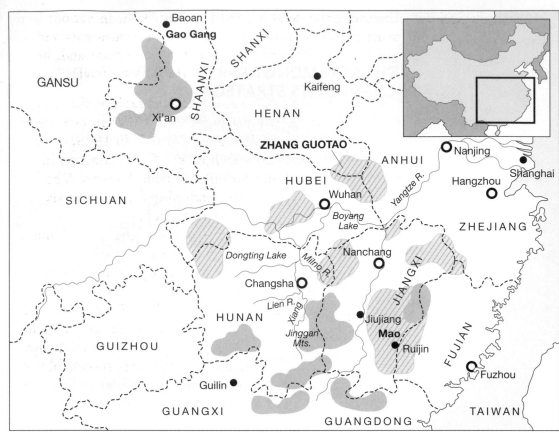

The Chinese Communist Party base areas and uprisings of 1927–28

supporters had been killed in the futile risings that had followed the Shanghai massacre and all that was left were a few isolated rural pockets in the more remote and inhospitable areas. Mao's group retreated from Hunan into the Jinggang mountains on the borders of Jiangxi province. Here Mao joined forces with the remnant of another failed rising in Nanchang. These troops were led by **Zhu De** and the army became known as the **Zhu–Mao Army**. Throughout 1928, it did more than survive. Its area of control expanded to cover half a million people. During this time, many of the basic principles on which the Maoist red armies were to operate with ultimate success were drawn up.

Pressure was however building up on Jinggang base and the forces retreated eastwards in early 1929 to another mountainous region on the Jiangxi Fujian border, around the town of Ruijin. This became the heart of the Central

KEY PERSON

Zhu De (1886–1976) was from a poor peasant family but showed great promise as a scholar. He became a soldier, policeman, criminal and drug addict. After being cured of addiction in 1922, he went to study in Germany where he became a Communist. On his return as an ex-professional soldier, he rapidly became the leader of one of the small communist armies and led the hopeless assault on the city of Nanchang in 1927.

KEY TERM

Zhu–Mao Army Many of the tactics and approaches of the much larger Red Army of 1946 evolved in 1928-29. Mao took the old saying of a famous bandit leader and applied it.

Guidelines were also laid down to be courteous and fair to the peasants.

KEY TERMS

Right deviationism is a phrase from the Soviet Union. The jargon was current at the time and used by Stalin and his supporters to describe those who opposed the policy of collectivisation and wanted instead to maintain the system of peasant agriculture.

Communist base area until October 1934. In various other parts of rural China, communist groups survived, but the Zhu–Mao one was the most important and, in November 1931, was named as the Central Soviet.

The period after 1927 was a period of rapidly changing leadership for the party. Chen Duxiu fell from power and was denounced as a follower of Trotsky. In 1928, it was felt to be too dangerous to hold the Party Congress in China and it was held 40 miles outside Moscow. The figures who dominated the leadership for the next six years were known as 'the returned Bolsheviks'. The leadership operated in secret from Shanghai until January 1933. The party argued hotly over the relative importance of an urban or rural strategy, the relationship of military force to the masses and the degree of dominance exercised by Moscow and the Comintern. Mao was never pre-eminent, but he was a significant figure as a full member of the Central Committee from 1928 and with Zhu the leading member of the most successful rural base.

The Jiangxi base area

Despite repeated attempts by the GMD government to destroy the Jiangxi base, it flourished and expanded. Mao as Base Area Party Secretary attempted to learn about more of the rural world he governed. In 1930, an analysis of one particular county was carried out recording in extraordinary detail the patterns of everyday life: who owned what; who ate what; who sold what. Peasants in debt sold their children, and in the county town of 2,684 inhabitants, there were 30 prostitutes. Land distribution was undertaken and the richer gentry either killed or driven off, but Mao had learned from his experiences in JingganJshan and sought to avoid alienating the richer peasants, who were often the most productive and most influential in a community. Against the wishes of the party purists in hiding in Shanghai, Mao insisted that the richer peasants were not class enemies but members of the progressive alliance against landlords This led to accusations of **right deviationism**.

Mao also seems to have devoted time to promoting rights for women. A new marriage law was issued in December 1931 outlawing arranged marriages and marriage through sale or purchase. Divorce was made easier. In spite of this, communist military units had 'teams of laundresses' attached to them and their duties included more than washing. Mao himself had taken a second wife, He Zizhen in 1928. His original wife had been left with the children in Changsha and at the time he claimed that she might have been executed. She was, but not until 1930 when she was publicly beheaded following a communist attack.

Armed conflict between the GMD and the CCP

The struggle between the GMD and the Communists was marked by unbelievable brutality on both sides. A series of encirclement campaigns was launched and the first three beaten off by Mao and Zhu De. The attacks were also marked by vicious purging of suspected agents within. This began on a large scale in 1930 with thousands accused of being **AB Tuans.** Those accused were tortured until they confessed to being GMD agents. The purges went on into 1931. Four hundred officers and men from the 20th Army were killed in 1931. The best estimate today is that tens of thousands were maimed and butchered. Mao himself used it to destroy rivals and cement his authority over local Communists.

Mao looked to be increasingly important, and in November 1931, following the defeat of the third encirclement campaign, the base area was declared to be the Chinese Soviet Republic; Mao was appointed State Chairman and head of government. In some ways, his power was to prove illusory. The GMD captured a senior Russian trained agent of the Communist Party who defected and betrayed thousands of Communists in the cities. The communist leadership in Shanghai decided to move to Jiangxi. Zhou Enlai arrived in 1932 and ousted Mao from his military positions. The rest of the leadership arrived in 1933 with a new Comintern military expert, Otto Braun, a German communist. Mao, despite his nominal position, was sidelined, and the real decisions taken by Zhou, Braun and the most important of the returned Bolsheviks **Bo Gu.** Land policies were made more extreme in line with those being practised in the Soviet Union. In reality, this meant the persecution of wealthier more successful peasants, contrary to Mao's

KEY TERM

AB Tuans were those accused of being secret GMD members. Because of the mixture and cooperation between the parties before 1927, it was a charge easy to make. It was, in reality, a form of paranoia at a time of great danger, when enemies could be believed to be lurking anywhere. The torture of suspects stopped only with confession. Most confessed. It had the great advantage to the leaders like Mao of reinforcing their authority, even though it probably killed more Communists than the GMD.

KEY PERSON

Bo Gu (1907–46) was one of the returned Bolsheviks and the dominant figure in the party from 1932 to 1935. He was very much under the influence of Moscow and the Comintern agent Otto Braun.

opinions. The result, as Mao had foreseen, was the loss of support.

Coinciding with the arrival of the top leadership, Chiang also advised by a German of a very different persuasion to Braun, General Hans von Seeckt, launched his fourth and fifth suppression campaigns. New roads and 14,000 blockhouses were built and the Soviet area was slowly strangled as the nationalist armies closed in. In consultation with Zhu, but not Mao, the decision was taken to abandon the Jiangxi area. The result was the Long March.

The Long March, 1934–35

On the night of 16th October 1934, approximately 80,000 Communists started to cross the Gan River and break out westwards towards Guangxi province. The planning was largely that of Zhou Enlai. Two military corps led the break-out, one under the 27-year-old Lin

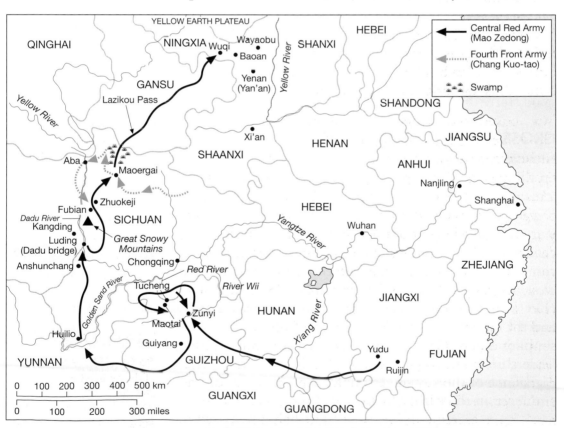

The Long March

Biao, and a slightly smaller one of 13,000 under Peng Dehuai. Mao went with the central command column. He took his pregnant second wife with him but left his two-year-old son behind. He was never to see him again.

Zhou and Zhu De chose the spot for breakout well. Chiang's best troops were advancing on the north side of the base area and on the south-west front the Communists faced poorly motivated warlord troops. Zhou had also entered into negotiations with the warlord governor of Guandong province and agreed a non-aggression pact and the provision of medical supplies in return for the rapid transit of the Communists. The Governor did not want to give Chiang an excuse for interference in his area. This illustrates just how fragile the unity of Republican China was. In many ways, it was a federation of semi-independent states and Chiang's writ did not effectively run further than his Yangtze stronghold area around Nanjing. A recent biographer of Mao has suggested that Chiang did not wish to destroy the Communists, but wanted merely to move them on. All the evidence seems to point against this and it was merely his lack of effective local control, not lack of determination, which allowed the Communists to make a good start.

CROSSING RIVERS AND MOUNTAINS

Chiang made a determined effort to stop the Communists on the Xiang River, on the border of Hunan. He inflicted a major defeat in a week-long battle at the beginning of December. The Communists lost much of their baggage and possibly half their numbers. They also decided to change direction and instead of trying to link up with communist forces in Hunan, moved into Guizhou to the west. Here GMD control was minimal. The great Wu river was crossed on bamboo rafts on 7th January 1935 and the city of Zunyi captured, with much-needed supplies of food. Here an important meeting of the top leadership of the party was held. The **Zunyi Conference** marks one of the key stages in Mao Zedong's rise to pre-eminence in the party.

Under Mao's guidance, the communist columns now made a bewildering number of changes of direction to escape pursuing GMD forces and local warlords in

KEY EVENT

The **Zunyi Conference** was held on 15–18th January 1935. It considered the mistakes that had led to the abandoning of the Jiangxi base and the defeat on the Xiang river. Bo Gu and his Comintern military adviser Braun were the chief losers. Mao was appointed a full member of the ruling Standing Committee of the Politburo.

Zhang Guotao (1897– 1979) was, like Mao, a founding member of the CCP in 1921. Like Mao, he had retreated after 1927 to founding a rural soviet in the north of China on the Hubei-Henan border. Even more than the Jiangxi Soviet, it stressed the liberation of women and progressive social policies. Forced out of the area by GMD pressure, Zhang moved to Sichuan in a rather shorter but more successful version of the Long March. He was an obvious rival to Mao but could not shake Mao's grip on the Politburo. He defected to the GMD in 1938 after losing a renewed power struggle with Mao in Ya'nan and eventually died in Canada, three years after Mao.

KEY EVENT

Crossing of the Dadu River The river was a formidable barrier and was a rushing flood from melting snow. A few boats were seized but not enough to ferry many men across. Mao ordered troops a hundred miles upstream to seize an old 120-yard (110 metres) chain bridge at Luding. Planks had been removed to make it unusable.

Guizhou, Yunnan and southern Sichuan. They swung far to the south and then turned north, finally crossing the upper Yangtze where least expected at the beginning of May. They ensured limited pursuit by moving all boats for a hundred miles to the north side. At the little town of Huili, the decision was taken to head north into north Sichuan and join forces with another communist column under **Zhang Guotao.**

What now followed was the most extraordinary and heroic phase of the march as this column of ragged southern Chinese made their way painfully into the cold upland plateaus of western China. One of the most famed events is the **crossing of the Dadu River** on 25th May, later much celebrated in communist propaganda but denied recently as never having taken place in Jung Chang and Jon Halliday's book, *Mao: The Untold Story* (2005).

A scene from a tapestry depicting Mao Tse-Tung on the Long March through China, 1935

Having crossed the Dadu, Mao decided to move north east over the Great Snow Mountains, over 4,260 metres high. Mao was suffering from malaria and had to be carried at times, as was his wife, recently hit by strafing from a GMD aircraft. On 12th June, they met with Zhang Guotao's force, numbering around 50,000, three times the remnant that was left of Mao's forces. The result was a power struggle between the two rather than cooperation. Mao wished to head north east to Gansu, but the way lay across a fearsome bog, 50 miles across, near to a horseshoe bend of the upper Yellow River. Zhang wished to head west to a safer area and away from nationalist power. After much argument they parted.

The crossing of the icy marshlands, 3,353 metres above sea level, was probably the most arduous part of the march. It was a stinking, freezing swamp with water unfit to drink on every side. Diarrhoea became rampant and food in short supply. Men picked grain from the bloody faeces left by their dying comrades. Men slept standing up during the six-day crossing of the swamp. Many were left in the morning too weak to move and drowned or froze to death. Reaching the north side, the heroic survivors defeated a force of GMD troops, sent by Chiang to head them off and, in one last memorable battle, stormed an apparently impregnable fortress guarding a crucial pass They entered Gansu province, and Mao learned of a small communist Soviet base area in Shaanxi province 600 miles to the north. On 22nd October 1935, they reached the impoverished cave village of Bao'an in northern Shaanxi, its weird lunar landscape dominated by dusty dark yellow loess.

It was semi-desert and the harvests failed frequently, but for the next 12 years it was to be the new communist bastion. The Long March was declared at an end. Perhaps 5,000 or 6,000 of the original 80,000–85,000 Communists had made it. As an heroic myth, it was later used to boost support for the Communist Party, but at the time it appeared to represent an almost unmitigated defeat.

'THE DISEASE OF THE SKIN': JAPAN AND CHINA, 1931–37

If Britain had seemed the most dangerous and aggressive of the foreign powers initially, by the twentieth century, Japan had assumed that role, inflicting humiliation after humiliation on the weakened Chinese state. Japan had taken over the German concessions in Shandong in 1919 and was well established in Manchuria, with control of the south Manchurian Railroad. The Old Marshal, Zhang

Zuolin, warlord of Manchuria was regarded as a friendly client. In the early and mid-1920s, Japan appeared content with the position of dominance that it had achieved and even made some concessions to Chinese pride.

Between 1928 and 1930, this approach changed to one of renewed aggression. A combination of circumstances both inside Japan and China explains this. The unification of China under the GMD and growing Chinese nationalism seemed potentially threatening. The bloody clash between Chiang's forces and the Japanese in Jinan in 1928 has already been mentioned. The attempt to replace the Old Marshal with his more malleable son had backfired and Manchuria had come under at least nominal GMD control. Japan was particularly hurt by the onset of the world slump in 1929 and her trade harmed by the growing protectionism, triggered by the USA. The answer seemed to lie in Manchuria, rich in minerals and arable land. It was relatively underpopulated in contrast to Japan and could be seen as a solution to Japan's economic problems as both a place for settlement and colonisation and a source of raw materials. Japan's civilian

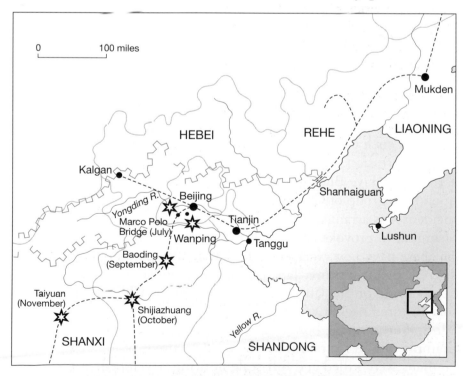

The war against the Japanese in northern China

government did not exercise much control over the Japanese army units stationed in south Manchuria and Korea and the result was the infamous **Mukden incident** of 18th September 1931.

The incident was used as a pretext to establish effective Japanese rule throughout Manchuria. Without orders from the Tokyo government, which was urging restraint, the Japanese commander in Korea sent troops across the border to join with those units already in the south of Manchuria and destroy any vestige of rival Chinese authority.

Chiang was in the middle of his third encirclement campaign against the Communists and felt China could not as yet confront Japan. He ordered the Young Marshal to withdraw his forces south of the Great Wall. China appealed to the League of Nations, who set up a Commission of Inquiry under Lord Lytton. Japan set up what it claimed was the independent state of Manchukuo, under the nominal headship of Pu Yi, the last Qing Emperor. When the League Commission reported in 1933, and did not accept the total loss of Chinese sovereignty, Japan walked out of the League of Nations and proceeded to intimidate China into agreement.

Although Chiang felt unable to confront Japan militarily in 1931, there was widespread public outrage. There was an extensive boycott of all Japanese products, cutting sales in China by two-thirds. This certainly hurt Japan at a time of such economic misery, and Japan declared it an act of aggression. The conflict now spread to Shanghai in early 1932. Five Buddhist monks from Japan were set upon by a group of Chinese. In reality, it appears that the incident was arranged by the Japanese military attaché in Shanghai to provoke conflict. He certainly succeeded. The Japanese navy now wanted to show that they could be as aggressive as the army. Japanese marines landed and began firing on the Chapei district of the city. Chinese soldiers fired back. On 29th January, the Japanese admiral ordered the bombing of the district, the first example of a terror raid from the air. Hundreds of civilians were killed and full-scale fighting developed. Seventy thousand Japanese troops were rushed to

KEY EVENT

The **Mukden incident (September 1931)** was the trigger for the Japanese conquest of Manchuria. It was the work of the local Kwantung Army in the south of Manchuria with the connivance of the Japanese army in Korea. Knowing that the government in Tokyo was sending a senior general to demand restraint, a group of junior officers struck first. They placed explosives along a section of the railway line close to the nearest Chinese barracks and blew up a section of track, blaming it on the Chinese. Fighting began and the Japanese seized the city of Mukden.

Shanghai. Throughout February 1932 a full-scale war raged causing massive damage to the city. The cost was put at US$1.5 billion by the city authorities. There was international outrage and, on 3rd March, an armistice was agreed. Japanese and Chinese troops withdrew from the city, but Chinese armed police remained. Japan had gained little but opprobrium in Shanghai, but she had secured Manchuria.

CONCLUSION

Over the next few years, Japanese power was slowly extended in the north with one concession after another forced from the Nanjing government. The Chinese accepted Japanese control of Manchuria in May 1933 under the **Treaty of Tanggu** and a demilitarised zone between the Great Wall and Beijing. Parts of inner Mongolia were seized and agreed to by Chiang and, in June 1935, China agreed to remove all troops from Hebei province. The question was when would China and Chiang resist. Chiang's view was to resist when the communist menace had been eliminated, but many of his own supporters disagreed.

Generalissimo Chiang was staying just outside the ancient city of **Xi'an** on 12th December 1936. He had arrived to supervise the encirclement and destruction of the Communists in neighbouring Shaanxi province. Early in the morning, with Chiang still in his nightshirt, his villa was attacked. Clad in his night attire and without his false teeth, he escaped over a 3-metre high wall and lay hidden on a nearby hillside for several hours. Frozen nearly to death, he finally surrendered to a group of soldiers, whom he discovered were working on the orders of the Young Marshal, Zhang Xueliang.

Zhang had been placed in charge of the anti-communist drive, which he had conducted very half-heartedly. His decision to seize Chiang was the result of a mixture of motives. He feared dismissal, but like several of the other northern commanders, he felt Chiang had his priorities wrong. The Japanese, not the Communists, should be the number one target. Already he had had secret talks with Zhou Enlai and wanted to recreate the United Front. Chiang proved difficult, telling his captors to shoot him

The **Treaty of Tanggu (May 1933)** was another in a long line of national humiliations. The Chinese delegation was led to a waiting Japanese delegation, deliberately chosen to be of inferior standing to the Chinese delegates. Under the guns of Japanese warships anchored nearby, the Chinese delegates were ordered to sign, and their protest that the agreement related only to a military truce not a political recognition of Manchukuo, went unrecorded.

if they wished. Mao and the Communists were overjoyed at the news of the capture and had they been there would have urged Zhang to take Chiang's invitation up immediately. This was until they heard from Moscow. Stalin insisted that the kidnapping was probably a Japanese plot and that Chiang was vital to Moscow's interests. Zhang realised as threats came in from other generals that only Chiang could be the national focus for resistance to Japan. Twelve difficult days of negotiation followed and Zhou Enlai met Chiang for the first time since they worked together at Whampoa in 1924–26. Without actually signing a formal agreement, Chiang gave the clear impression that he would change his priorities. He was released and greeted in Nanjing by huge crowds of enthusiastic Chinese, clearly anxious for national salvation and resistance to the Grey Dragon: Japan.

SUMMARY QUESTIONS

1 What were the achievements and failures of Chiang Kaishek in the years 1927–37?

2 Why did the GMD regime of Chiang Kaishek fail to destroy the CCP in the years 1927–37?

3 Should the Long March be considered a triumph or a disaster for the CCP?

4 In what ways did Japan weaken the GMD regime in the years 1931–37?

TIMELINE	
1928	Second Northern Expedition; Chiang gains Beijing; Mao establishes the Jiangxi base area
1931	Japanese seize Manchuria
1932–33	Communist leadership withdraws from Shanghai to Jiangxi
October 1934	Long March begins
October 1935	Long March ends
1936	Chiang kidnapped at Xi'an; second United Front

CHAPTER 5

War with Japan

INTRODUCTION

Europeans think of the Second World War as beginning in 1939 with the German attack on Poland. In Asia, the Second World War began two years earlier in the summer of 1937. This event is of enormous importance for both China and the world as a whole. In the short term, it brought appalling suffering to millions of Chinese men and women. It saved the Communists and ultimately helped them to victory throughout China. Mao, towards the end of his life, was to make this point to a visiting Japanese Prime Minister in the 1970s. It eventually helped to precipitate US entry into the war in 1941, thereby determining the defeat of Japan and Germany in 1945.

THE OUTBREAK OF WAR, JULY 1937

The outbreak of full-scale conflict in the summer of 1937 was probably an accident, in the sense that neither side's governments sought a full-scale war at that time. It was nevertheless the inevitable consequence of the Japanese determination to achieve dominance in north-east China and the impossibility of Chiang's government to accept any further humiliations. Like so many momentous events in human history, a complex interplay of apparently trivial incidents produced something of enormous significance, which was to bring misery and death to millions.

The indecisive Prince Konoe had just taken over as Prime Minister in Japan and the senior commanding Japanese general in northern China had had a heart attack leading to his replacement with an inexperienced colleague. Shortly afterwards on 7th July, a clash occurred between Japanese soldiers on a night exercise and Chinese troops around a famous bridge 10 miles west of Beijing. This was the **Marco Polo Bridge incident**. In Japan, a major debate ensued between those anxious to avoid conflict and the hardliners who saw the escalating clashes as an

Marco Polo Bridge incident The bridge was a famous landmark and known to westerners as the Marco Polo Bridge on account of the Venetian's description of it in the thirteenth century. Japanese troops were entitled to be in the area under the Boxer Protocol and do not appear to have been looking for trouble. In the course of a night exercise, they temporarily lost a soldier, who subsequently turned up. He appears to have stopped to urinate or to have fallen. The Japanese went in search of him and clashed with nearby Chinese forces and rifle fire was exchanged. Although a local cease fire was arranged, clashes between Japanese and Chinese forces around Beijing multiplied in July 1937.

opportunity to seize control of northern China. On 26th July, the hardliners won and the Chinese were given an ultimatum to withdraw all forces from Beijing. The Japanese then occupied Beijing and attacked several neighbouring towns, in one of which, Donzhou, Japanese troops killed every civilian they could find. Japanese reinforcements were rushed to northern China.

Normally, such developments had been followed by Chinese concessions and an armistice. This time, Chiang announced that 'the limits of endurance had been reached'. A national conference was held, which Zhou Enlai attended for the Communists. Mao in Yan'an declared a policy of 'total resistance by the whole nation'. The war had come sooner than Chiang would have liked, but he had to fight or face his own replacement. His strategic decision now transformed the conflict.

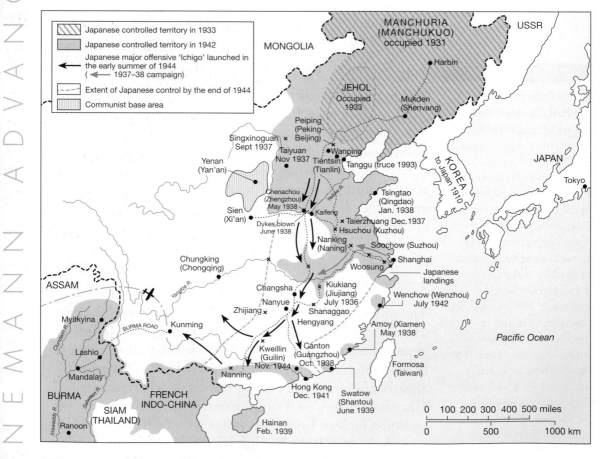

The war with Japan

The Japanese had imagined a limited conflict in the north with the commitment of a maximum of 250,000 troops. Chiang now transformed the war by extending it to the Yangtze valley. He decided on a bold move, to attack the Japanese forces in Shanghai where the best part of his German-trained army was. This was to lead to military disaster for the Chinese and a massive escalation of the war, but it also sucked the Japanese into a conflict they did not want and absorbed far more of their army and resources than they could afford. It ultimately contributed to their defeat. The clear winners from this strategy in the long term were the Communists in the north, who were able to survive and expand as the Japanese bogged themselves down in the centre and Chiang's regime suffered military defeat after defeat.

THE FIGHT FOR SHANGHAI, AUGUST – NOVEMBER 1937

The Chinese attack began with a terrible own goal. On 14th August, Chiang ordered his new Italian-trained air force to bomb Japanese warships anchored off Shanghai. Bad luck played a part with the arrival of an unexpected typhoon, but for whatever reason the bombs dropped, missed the Japanese entirely and hit various parts of Shanghai including buildings within the French Concession, which suffered devastating damage. Over a thousand civilians were killed. It was merely the start of the city's nightmare. Chiang's troops attacked the area held by the Japanese near to the shore and where the Japanese were landing troops. The Chinese failed to break through and the Japanese rushed in reinforcements, a further 15 divisions to northern and central China. They used their naval units to shell the city. Bitter fighting took place throughout September and October. Chiang lost more than 250,000 men as dead or wounded. These were his best troops. The Japanese suffered 40,000–70,000 casualties, far more than they anticipated. In the light of their losses and the almost total air supremacy of the Japanese, provided by aircraft carriers and planes from Taiwan, the Chinese began to withdraw in November. Defensive positions had been prepared to block a Japanese advance towards Nanjing if things went wrong in Shanghai.

THE RAPE OF NANJING, DECEMBER 1937 – JANUARY 1938

The defeated Chinese army retreating from Shanghai, failed to hold the defensive positions at Wuxi on the railroad to Nanjing. Chiang and his government decided to withdraw to Wuhan, leaving 90,000 troops under an opium-smoking ex-warlord to defend the city. After three days of artillery and air attacks, the general fled as did most of the troops that could get away. On 13th December, Japanese troops entered Nanjing. What followed was the recreation of hell. Every vile, perverted torture that man can devise to abase and injure another human being was practised by the Japanese on the Chinese inhabitants. Two Japanese sub-lieutenants entered into a competition to see who could behead the first hundred victims. Reaching a hundred each, they went on. Civilians were hung up by their tongues, buried alive, used for bayonet practice and sprayed with acid. Women were multiply raped, many to death. Age was no defence. Old women of 80 were attacked as were pre-teen girls. Babies were tossed in the air to be caught on bayonets. Estimates inevitably vary as to the total number of victims, but somewhere in the region of 300,000 is possible. A moving account is provided by Iris Chang in *The Rape of Nanking: The Forgotten Holocaust of World War II* (1997). The Japanese have never fully accepted the horror of these seven weeks. It must stand with the Holocaust as one of the real monuments to human bestiality.

Japanese atrocities during the rape of Nanjing in 1937–38

THE WAR IN 1938 AND RETREAT TO CHONGQING

Bitter fighting continued through the winter. The Japanese advanced from the north and up the Yangtze valley, their objective the great tri-city of Wuhan. On the border of Shandong province in April, one of Chiang's best generals gave the Japanese a bloody nose. In a brilliant feinted retreat into the old walled town of Taierzhuang, Li Zongren drew the Japanese after him and then sprang a trap, killing 8,000 in the town and many more outside. It was a heartening victory for the Chinese and showed that when well led and motivated as these Guanxi troops were, a Chinese army could beat the invader. It was, however, all too symptomatic of the situation in the army that Chiang did not trust Li and kept a secret female agent in Li's headquarters to report on plots.

The Chinese victory provided only a temporary respite, and the important railway junction of Xuzhou fell to the Japanese in May. This was near to where Li had won his victory. The Guanaxi general carried out a skilful withdrawal. To try to save the situation, Chiang ordered a desperate remedy: the dikes holding the Yellow River to its course were blown in June. The river reverted to its old route to the sea, i.e. that before 1853 and flooded thousands of hectares, destroying 4,000 villages and drowning thousands. No warning was given. It left a legacy of bitterness that was to reduce support for the Nationalist Party (GMD) regime after the war. In 1938, it held up the Japanese advance for three months.

Chiang was also helped by Stalin. Soviet planes with Russian pilots were sent to assist the nationalist forces and even more worrying for the Japanese, **a series of clashes with the Red Army** developed on the frontiers of Manchuria. Despite the flooding and Soviet assistance, the Japanese still took Wuhan in October and a few days before, seized Canton in a sea-borne invasion. This had the effect of sealing off Chiang's regime from direct commercial contact with the outside world. The Japanese hoped that this would induce surrender and dependency on Japan. In October, Chiang withdrew from Wuhan even further up the Yangtze. This time he moved his capital far inland beyond the dramatic Yangtze gorges to the cloud-covered Chongqing in Sichuan. There would be no surrender.

The Japanese were already massively over extended and worried by the tensions with the Russians on the frontiers of Manchuria. Chiang had drawn them into a much more

KEY EVENT

A **series of clashes with the Red Army** developed on the frontiers of Manchuria. Japanese strategy appeared to be geared to an assault on Russia in Asia. Japan signed the Anti-Comintern Pact with Germany and Italy and made a series of provocative pushes on the frontier of Manchuria. In July and August 1938, there was five weeks of intermittent fighting. The Japanese were pushed back. The Russian troops were commanded by Marshal Blyucher, whom Chiang knew as Galen and still held in high regard since their cooperation in the 1920s. Stalin, however, did not hold Blyucher in high regard. A week after he defeated the Japanese, Blyucher was recalled to Moscow, arrested by the NKVD, and eventually shot. A further clash took place in 1939 with the Japanese again defeated. They began to reconsider their strategy of confronting Russia.

extensive conflict in central China than they had intended. They tried to set up cooperative puppet regimes in the areas occupied on the model of Manchukuo. In Inner Mongolia, a Mongol prince, reputedly descended from Ghenghis Khan, was installed. In what was left of Nanjing, an old rival of Chiang in the GMD was placed in nominal control. The reality in all areas was Japanese control, exploitation and cruelty. Large numbers of troops were required as an occupation force. When war came between Japan and the USA and Britain in December 1941, 34 out of 50 divisions were in China and Manchuria. By the end of 1938, China seemed to have totally lost the unity that Chiang had worked for ten years to achieve. There were three main areas: nationalist China based in Chonqing, communist China based in Shaanxi and Japanese-occupied China in the east and north. But the Japanese-occupied area was fragmented into sub-divisions like Manchukuo, and Chiang only had nominal control over much of the area that was still free of Japanese troops.

In 1939 and 1940, the Japanese merely sought to consolidate their hold on the eastern seaboard and pacify the areas they were holding. The war with nationalist China became a series of raids into what was a very wide no-man's land. Bombing raids were carried out frequently on Chonqing, but no killer blow was delivered.

COMMUNIST CHINA AND THE TRIUMPH OF MAO

In January 1937, the communist leaders moved to Yan'an, which was to be the seat of their power for the next ten years. Mao was the dominant but not unchallenged leader. He faced a renewed challenge from Zhang Guotao, which ended with the latter's defection in 1938 to the GMD, and a more dangerous one from a newly returned Bolshevik, Wang Ming, who arrived from Moscow in November 1937. He had been head of the Chinese section of the Comintern and had been sent back to ensure the smooth working of the United Front, on which Stalin set much store. Mao accepted the need for cooperation but also the need for a clearly separate identity, and in the light of past experience, a healthy

KEY TERMS

The **rectification campaign** began in 1942 and was a process of consolidating the party behind Mao. For most senior figures, it meant confession of past errors and public acknowledgement of the correctness of Mao's thought. The strong-arm tactics were provided by Kang Sheng, an NKVD-trained operative. He smoked out GMD agents and was given a free hand to employ torture and physical abuse for a while by Mao. This led to criticism and, in August 1943, he was reined in. It was later admitted that many innocent party members had been accused and were now pardoned. Unfortunately, many were dead.

The **General Will** see page 101

A **personality cult** developed in 1943 after Mao was declared Chairman of the Politburo. His deputy declared that the only way to prevent future errors was to ensure Mao's thought penetrated everywhere. The term Mao Zedong's Thought was coined at this time and the red anthem, *The East is Red* was written:

'*The East is Red, the sun rises,*
In China a Mao Zedong is born.
He seeks the people's happiness.
He is the people's saviour'

suspicion of Chiang and the GMD. Like all great politicians, Mao's strength lay in balancing between positions. With regard to the Soviet Union, he recognised its importance but remained a Han Chinese first and foremost and this gave him popularity.

For Mao, Wang Ming was too much the creature of Moscow and too much the Marxist dogmatist. Mao had come to represent a distinctive Chinese Communism and this was accepted at an important Politburo meeting in September 1941. The errors of the returned Bolsheviks in bringing disaster between 1931 and 1935 were compared with the success since then. Mao's position was endorsed by all the leadership bar Wang and Bo Gu. Mao rubbed in his triumph more publicly in a speech to the Central Party School in February 1942 in the typical earthy language which so many of the humbler Chinese Communists could identify with.

> *Your dogma is of less use than dog-shit. Dog-shit can fertilise fields and man's shit can feed dogs. But dogmas? They can't fertilise fields and they can't feed dogs.*

The speech marked the onset of the **rectification campaign.** This cemented Mao's hold on the party. Opponents were pressured into confessing past mistakes and publicly humiliated. Some suffered torture but nothing on the scale of the earlier campaign against AB Tuans. Mao's ideas came to be accepted as central for right-thinking party members. At the heart lay a Chinese version of Rousseau's concept of the **General Will**. Mao was widely read in western philosophy and distilled the thoughts of others into something relevant to China's mid-twentieth century situation He stressed that all ideas had to come from the masses but within the masses it was inchoate. The role of the Communist Party was to formulate these vague ideas into practical beliefs and policies and return with them to the masses: 'This is what you were thinking.' Mao himself showed unbounded self-confidence and it was this, together with a ruthless skill as a political operator, that carried him to the top of the party. **A personality cult** developed in the latter stages of the war and at the Seventh Party Congress in 1945, Mao was declared Chairman of the whole party.

He was clearly number one and his deputy was Liu Shaoqi. Zhou Enlai was number three, but he had had to make extensive self-criticism. He had been wrong in the past; Mao had been right. The little boy who had confronted his father years before and got his way was now the master of the party and no opposition was to be tolerated.

The expanding of the party

The party really had expanded dramatically helped by a mixture of policies and events. At a conference in Wayaobu held on Christmas Day 1935, Mao's flexible approach to party recruitment had been endorsed. 'Left closed doorism' was out. Even the rich bourgeoisie should be allowed to join in the struggle for a new China and to defeat the Japanese. Party membership increased from 40,000 in 1937 to 800,000 by 1940 and 1.2 million by 1945. The army grew from 22,000 in early 1936 to half a million in 1940 and 880,000 in 1945. Not only was there the 8th Route Army of Shaanxi and the north under Zhu and Peng Dehuai, but in the old base areas of the south that had been abandoned in the Long March, the remnants left behind had formed themselves into the New 4th Army. Within the Japanese-controlled north, communist-controlled guerrilla groups sprang up. The Communists were increasingly seen as the real hope of a new China as the nationalist regime suffered defeat after defeat.

Mao's policies proved popular. Gentry and landlord extermination was replaced by a policy of rent limitation and reduction. In those areas controlled by the party there were drives to stamp out corruption and promote literacy. The growing party bureaucracy was encouraged to help and strengthen village life and promote the rural economy. This was all part of Mao's grand strategy of winning over the masses. It seemed to be working.

The Japanese remained a serious military headache. A minor military victory was won by Lin Biao in 1937, the first Chinese military victory of the war. Deng Xiaoping and the 129th Division established a forward base in the mountains of eastern Shanxi. Mao was suspicious of straightforward conventional attacks on foes as formidable as the Japanese, but in 1940 the Hundred Regiment offensive was launched in August and went on to December. It inflicted many casualties on the Japanese but even more on the Communists and many more on the civilian population. The Japanese retaliated with their customary brutality. The 'Three All' campaign was launched: kill all, burn all, loot all.

Relations between the Communists and GMD, never good, deteriorated rapidly in 1941. Fearful of the growth in communist power, Chiang attacked the New 4th Army in the south on the grounds that the Communists should not operate south of the Yangtze, and when ordered north, they had refused. Thousands of communist troops were killed by Nationalists in January. It did not destroy the New 4th Army, which regrouped to the north and even left behind guerrilla cells in the south which multiplied. It provided useful propaganda for the Communists who could point to their sacrifices against the common enemy and the treachery of the GMD.

The widening war – Uncle Sam to the rescue

The US entry into the war transformed the situation. Tension between the USA and Japan had been rising since the extended conflict in China began but worsened perceptibly in 1940. Japan had signed the Tri-Partite Pact with Germany and Italy in September of that year aimed against the USA. The USA was beginning to employ economic sanctions against Japan to force her to moderate her aggression in China, banning the export of scrap metal in September. Following the Japanese occupation of French Indo-China in July 1941, the USA imposed an oil embargo as well. The Dutch and British followed suit. This would ultimately bring the Japanese war machine to a halt. Japan decided to seize the resources needed by occupying the Dutch East Indies. To prevent US or British interference the decision was made to strike against the main US naval base in Hawaii and the British base in Singapore. On 7th December, a Sunday, the Japanese struck the US fleet in Pearl Harbor, before declaring war.

Chiang like most other people realised that Japan would now ultimately be defeated. All he needed to do was hold out. US aid now became available. The problem was how to get it to Chongqing. The only way was via 600 miles of dirt road from Burma. This was cut by the Japanese occupation of Burma in April 1942. Until a new route could be created from north-east India, known as the Ledo Road, the only answer was **the Hump.**

US military assistance

The Americans provided more than just supplies. Chiang accepted a US Chief of Staff, Lieutenant General Joseph Stillwell, known as 'Vinegar Joe'. Although a fluent Chinese speaker, Stillwell's relationship with Chiang was not an easy one. He was outraged by the incompetence of many of Chiang's appointees and privately referred to Chiang as 'the peanut'. He devoted most of his energy to building up a US-trained force which could recapture northern Burma and improve the supply position. He finally succeeded in this in August 1944. The clashes with Chiang grew and, in October 1944, Chiang secured his replacement with a less abrasive American, General Wedemeyer.

Another aspect of US assistance was the arrival of American air power under General Claire Chennault. In contrast to the buttoned-up and acerbic northerner, Stillwell, Chennault was an expansive southerner who got on very well with Madame Chiang. She, unlike her husband, spoke fluent English, although with an American accent. Chennault believed it to be possible to win the war from China through air power alone. He pressed for the build-up of the grandly titled 14th US Air Force. Initially, he argued that 12 heavy bombers stationed in China would do untold damage to the Japanese economy. In this, as in other things, he was to be disappointed. Nevertheless, throughout 1943 and early 1944 his air squadrons were built up. The arrival of the new super-bombers, the B29s, really did threaten Japan and Manchuria, and the Japanese responded as Stillwell had always argued they would. In April 1944, the Japanese launched their first major ground offensive against the Nationalists since 1938.

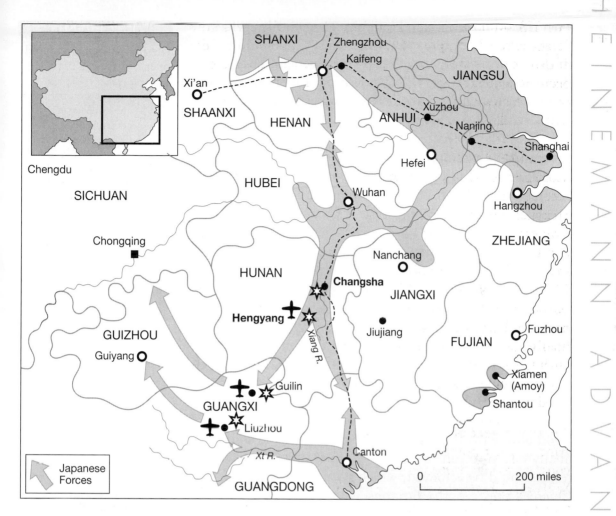

The Ichigo offensive, 1944

The Ichigo offensive

Ichigo was the Japanese code for their new offensive. They struck south towards the major US bases at Kweilin and Liuchow. Changsha fell without a fight, the Chinese 4th Army simply marching off to the south west. Time and time again, thousands of Chinese troops simply melted away before inferior forces of Japanese. The nationalist armies were riddled with problems from top to bottom. Chiang did not trust many of his generals and kept them short of equipment. Appointments to the best equipped units were based on loyalty to Chiang rather than competence. Officers embezzled pay and food and kept dead men on the books to claim their pay. It was an eye-opener for Chinese troops trained under Stillwell for his Burmese offensive that they were fed properly, trained with live ammunition and had proper medical services. Wedermeyer later remarked that many Chinese units like the 13th Army were 'more ready for a general hospital than the general reserve'. Malnutrition, tuberculosis and beriberi were widespread among new recruits. The Japanese, having achieved their objectives of occupying the vital airfields, halted their offensives. They were over-stretched and facing horrifying threats elsewhere as the Americans island hopped towards Japan itself. China had become a backwater, but the Ichigo campaign had done irreparable harm to the prestige of Chiang's regime.

CONCLUSION

Wedermeyer was preparing 39 Chinese divisions for an offensive eastwards to seize a major port, which would ease the supply position still further. Some Americans were already thoroughly disillusioned with Chiang and his regime. A small group had sought to make contact with the Communists and the so-called Dixie mission reached Yan'an in July 1944, much to the distaste of Chiang. The mission was duly impressed with the energy and aggression of the Communists and contrasted them favourably with the GMD. The offensive in the south finally began to roll in July 1945, but before decisive results could be achieved, which might have raised Chiang's prestige, the **Japanese surrendered**. One nightmare for the Chinese people had ended suddenly. Another was about to begin.

SUMMARY QUESTIONS

1 Why did a major conflict between Japan and China break out in the summer of 1937?

2 To what extent did the war with Japan weaken the regime of Chiang Kaishek?

3 In what ways did the war between China and Japan strengthen the CCP?

4 Why had Mao Zedong emerged as the unchallenged leader of the CCP by 1945?

The **Japanese surrendered** on 2nd September 1945. Japanese power collapsed suddenly in the summer of 1945. Most of Japan's fleet was destroyed at Leyte Gulf in October 1944. US submarines devastated her merchant marine and halted imports, and extensive bombing began. Tokyo was all but flattened in March 1945 with over 100,000 casualties. Russia declared war and invaded Manchuria on 8th August, just two days after the city of Hiroshima became the first recipient of nuclear attack. This was repeated on Nagasaki three days later. On 15th August, Japan announced that the country would accept unconditional surrender. In the words of the Emperor Hirohito, 'They would endure the unendurable'. The formal surrender took place on a US battleship in Tokyo Bay on 2nd September 1945.

July 1937 First clashes in the north

August 1937 Conflict spreads to Shanghai

December 1937 Rape of Nanjing

June 1938 Yellow river diverted to hold up Japanese

October 1938 Chiang retreats to Chongqing

1940 Communists launch Hundred Regiment offensive against the Japanese

1941 US entry into the war

1942 Rectification campaign strengthens Mao's hold on the CCP

1944 Japanese Ichigo offensive

1945 Japanese surrender

CHAPTER 6

Civil war and communist victory

INTRODUCTION

Between September 1945 and October 1949, the situation in China was transformed. Mao's Communists in their rural base areas firstly defended themselves from Chiang Kaishek's attempts to exterminate them and then moved on to the offensive and eventually drove Chiang and his Nationalist Party (GMD) regime from the mainland to exile in Taiwan. Mao's new communist government established a grip on the whole of China tighter than the Qing Emperors of the eighteenth century. The USSR half-heartedly backed the Communists expecting Chiang to win; the USA half-heartedly backed Chiang, well aware of his multiple weaknesses.

Mao and Chiang Kaishek in 1945

The international context is vital to explaining much of the behaviour of the USA and USSR in China during these years. Until September 1945, they had been allies. The USSR had received massive amounts of aid from the USA and privately, Soviet leaders admitted that Russia would have been defeated without it. The ending of the war produced tensions and the alliance slowly turned into the confrontation of the Cold War. This was a gradual and not a simple process but the result of growing misunderstandings and misconceptions. Stalin was nervous of US air power and its nuclear monopoly, and the Americans came to fear Soviet military power and expansion. In this they were encouraged by the British.

THE SITUATION IN AUGUST 1945

The war had certainly strengthened the communist position. When the Japanese surrendered, the

Communists had a membership of 1.2 million, approximately 900,000 soldiers under their command, and control of 19 base areas with a combined population of 90 million Their strength lay essentially north of the Yangtze. However, they lacked heavy military equipment such as artillery, of which they had only 600 pieces. They also had no air power, the component that the Second World War had revealed as vital to military success.

By comparison, Chiang and his GMD regime was regarded as the legitimate ruler of China by all the victors including the Soviet Union. China was even treated as a great power and given one of the permanent seats on the Security Council of the new United Nations. The foreign concessions had been ended by international agreement in 1943. Taiwan, lost to Japan in 1895, had been recovered. Chiang could boast that much of the nationalist agenda of his party had been achieved and all that was required was to establish complete control throughout China. To do this, the Communists had to be eliminated or rendered harmless as junior partners. Nationalist military power appeared overwhelming. Chiang had 2.7 million soldiers, admittedly many were poorly trained and motivated, but there were 39 divisions newly trained and armed by the Americans and these were formidable. His army had ten times the artillery of the Communists and an air force. If there were to be a conflict, it looked as if it would be very unequal.

The presence and aid of the USA, now the greatest power in the world, was also an important asset. The US General Wedemeyer was instructed by Washington to assist Chiang in moving his forces into key positions. Consequently, US Dakotas airlifted 110,000 Chinese troops to vital strategic points so that they could receive the Japanese surrenders. The only bright spot for the Communists was the large numbers of Russian troops in Manchuria who had now captured Japanese military supplies. The Russians did help the Communists achieve a dominance in Manchuria and handed over to them much of the stockpiled weapons and ammunition of the Japanese. From the arsenal at Shenyang (Mukden), the Red forces seized 100,000 guns and many thousands of artillery pieces. This much improved the fighting capacity of the Communist 8th Route Army, which was to be renamed the People's Liberation Army (PLA).

Even this silver lining was covered with a dark cloud. On the very day Japan had surrendered, Molotov, the Soviet foreign minister, had signed a treaty of alliance with Chiang's regime. It looked as if it was 1936 all over again. Stalin clearly saw a GMD China as much more likely and viable than a communist one. Stalin did not appear to want to confront the USA in China and preferred a neutral GMD government. The result of the international situation and pressure from both the USA and the Soviet Union was a series of negotiations between the Communists and the Nationalists to achieve union and preserve peace.

ATTEMPTS TO PREVENT CIVIL WAR, AUGUST 1945 – JUNE 1946

Mao was not keen to leave Yan'an and suggested Zhou handled the negotiations, but Chiang insisted on Mao attending. Under intense pressure from Stalin, Mao allowed himself to be flown by the Americans to Chongqing, but he insisted on the US ambassador coming to Yan'an and travelling with him as a guarantee against accidents. He refused Chiang's car at the airport and went with Patrick Hurley, the US ambassador. Such suspicion boded ill for the success of the talks.

While the talks were continuing, both sides rushed to improve their positions throughout the country. The Communists moved rapidly into Manchuria. At the talks, generalised agreements were reached about multi-party democracy and a need to avoid civil war, but detailed agreement proved impossible. The Communists offered to withdraw from south of the Yangtze but would not agree to Chiang's demand for control of their armies and local governments in the north. On 11th October 1945, Mao returned to Yan'an with nothing really settled, but he was deeply relieved to have escaped assassination.

The conflict rapidly escalated in November as nationalist forces began to move into Manchuria and 50,000 US marines occupied Beijing, Tianjin and other key points in the north to aid the GMD takeover. The communist commander in the north, the formidable **Lin Biao**, admitted that the key strategic town giving access to Manchuria was lost and could not be recaptured. The situation looked ominous for the Communists and was further worsened by the Russians. Stalin was worried by deteriorating relations with the USA worldwide and, as a gesture of friendship, proposed to cooperate with the Nationalists and hand over the Manchurian cities to Chiang. The Communists were ordered by the Russians to withdraw from the cities. This was another betrayal by Stalin. Mao seemed to suffer a health breakdown as he so often did when he could not see the political way forward. The idea of fighting the Nationalists fully backed by the USA and with the benevolent neutrality of the USSR was deeply unappealing. Mao was stumped and took to his bed. He was saved by US President Truman.

The arrival of George C Marshall

In an attempt to preserve peace and get the Russians out of Manchuria, Truman dispatched almost the most senior figure he could to try to settle China. **General George C Marshall** arrived in December 1945, and Mao breathed a sigh of relief. It would mean a halt to the nationalist offensive and, sure enough, a ceasefire was arranged and accepted by both sides in January 1946. Mao conceded the free movement of GMD forces. Chiang was forced to call a Political Consultative Conference to consider the future of China. A mixture of moderate GMD, independents and Communists took control away from Chiang and proceeded to map out a deal which Mao was prepared to accept. This involved a coalition government with communist participation. Agreement was even reached on the merger of the two armies. The Soviet Union began to withdraw from Manchuria.

THE UNRAVELLING OF THE DEAL AND THE PATH TO CIVIL WAR

The deal then unravelled. Chiang was determined not to accept parliamentary government. His position was like that of Yuan Shikai, believing that China needed some sort of autocratic government. His secret police began the assassination of his liberal critics. He persuaded the USA that he had to move his forces fully into Manchuria to avoid a communist seizure. Mao responded by ordering

Lin Biao (1908–71) was in many ways the outstanding soldier of the Chinese Revolution. He was a graduate of the Whampoa Military Academy under Chiang and served under him in the first Northern Expedition. He joined the Communist Party in 1927 and served with distinction in the Long March, being given command of the larger of two corps when only 27. At Yan'an, he headed the military academy. He became a member of the Central Committee in 1945. He was created a Marshal in 1955 and became defence minister in 1959. From 1966, he was Mao's appointed successor. He was killed in a plane crash in 1971.

General George C Marshall was the Chief of Staff throughout the Second World War, and as such the directing hand behind US strategy. After his unhappy term as Ambassador-envoy to China, President Truman appointed him Secretary of State, which position he held from 1947 to 1949. His experiences in China left him with a jaundiced view of Chiang's regime and anxious to avoid further involvement. Like many of his staff, he felt it to be pointless to back a regime which seemed incapable of reforming itself.

Lin Biao to launch a counter-attack and the Communists seized the city of Harbin as a base in the north of Manchuria. Lin was, however, told only to defend positions and not to provoke the Nationalists. Mao still hoped to isolate Chiang from moderates in the GMD and even more from the Americans. Unfortunately, the intensification of ill-feeling between the USSR and the USA in Europe enabled Chiang to drag a reluctant USA along. In June, a renewed nationalist assault took place. This was followed by one more last ditch ceasefire, which broke down the following month.

From July, Chiang's forces began an all-out assault on the communist position in the north. The USA, with deep reluctance, went along with it. Threats of cutting off aid were half-hearted and Chiang called Marshall's bluff. He was convinced that he could finish off the Communists, and the Americans would have to accept him as the only available friend. He was right; growing anti-Americanism was rife in China. The rape of a Chinese student by an American soldier in December 1946 led to **massive student protests**. The USA was increasingly seen as the one remaining imperialist power and, as such, the most resented. Marshall left in January 1947. He had failed in his main task, but at least the Russians had left Manchuria.

CIVIL WAR, JULY 1946 – NOVEMBER 1949

The first year was one of nationalist victories as their superior numbers, resources and air power told. Most of the cities of Manchuria were occupied except for Harbin and the far north. The communist leadership was even chased out of its old base of Yan'an. Mao was unperturbed. It was his old strategy of running away and circling around, drawing the enemy out to weaken him. He is reported as quoting the Analects of Confucius following the loss of Yan'an: 'If a thing comes to me and I give nothing in return, that is contrary to propriety.' Mao added: 'We give Chiang Yan'an. He will give us China.' It is significant that he quoted Confucius. Mao was much more a scholar of Chinese history and philosophy than a Marxist. Marxism might come in handy from time to time, but the lessons of Chinese history were more valuable.

KEY EVENT

Massive student protests became a feature of these years aimed against the Americans and later against the GMD regime itself. A student demonstration in July 1948 was met with considerable repression and resulted in the deaths of 14 students.

In Manchuria, a bitter conflict raged between Lin Biao and Chiang's best armies. GMD forces were increasingly cut off in the cities. Chiang had done little to win over the Manchu population but had alienated many by appointing cronies from the south to govern Manchuria and command the armies there. He missed the opportunity to use the influence of the Young Marshal in Manchuria. He was simply kept under house arrest, still not forgiven by Chiang for his part in the Xi'an incident of 1936. As so often in the past, Chiang's suspicions of his military colleagues had damaging effects. People's Liberation Army (PLA) forces and communist militia blew up the linking railways and deprived urban garrisons of supplies. Guerrilla attacks were accompanied by full conventional assaults in May 1947. Lin, without air cover, was beaten back, but the morale of GMD forces began to fail. In 1948, the Communists shifted fully to a policy of all-out assault. In a brilliant campaign Lin Biao destroyed much of the nationalist armies in Manchuria in a 31-hour battle. Chiang ignored US advice that he pull out his forces, which were isolated in Shen-yang and Jinan. He decided to try to hold on through air power, using aircraft to supply his beleaguered troops. He used up almost all of his military budget trying to maintain supplies. By November, Manchuria was lost and with it nearly half a million of Chiang's best troops.

Chiang's final stand

Chiang now attempted to make a stand near the crucial railway junction of Xuzhou in the south of Shandong province. Six hundred thousand troops on both sides faced each other. Commanded by Zhu De, Mao's veteran colleague, the Communists fought a classic positional battle relying on massed heavy artillery. Chiang showed a strategic incompetence in choosing an area of conflict where his forces could be attacked from three sides. As so often in the war against Japan, he could not refrain from interfering in the conduct of the battle from 200 miles away. Distrust of his military subordinates was a fatal weakness and contrasted with Mao, who provided the general framework and then left it to his generals to get on with it. The Communists enjoyed the help of 2 million peasant labourers mobilised by Deng Xiaoping.

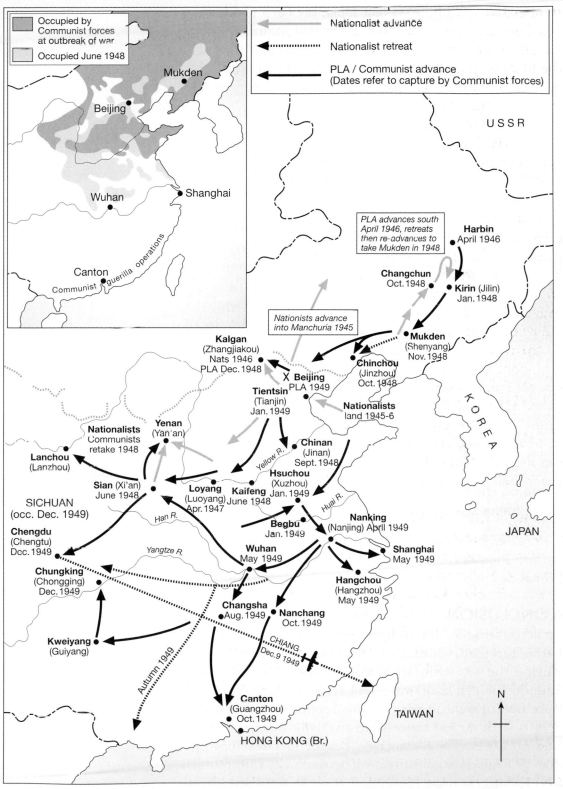

Map legend

Occupied by Communist forces at outbreak of war

Occupied June 1948

Nationalist advance

Nationalist retreat

PLA / Communist advance (Dates refer to capture by Communist forces)

Mukden

Beijing

Wuhan

Shanghai

Canton

Communist guerilla operations

USSR

PLA advances south April 1946, retreats then re-advances to take Mukden in 1948

Harbin April 1946

Changchun Oct. 1948

Kirin (Jilin) Jan. 1948

Nationists advance into Manchuria 1945

Mukden (Shenyang) Nov. 1948

Kalgan (Zhangjiakou) Nats 1946 PLA Dec. 1948

Chinchou (Jinzhou) Oct. 1948

X Beijing PLA 1949

Tientsin (Tianjin) Jan. 1949

Nationalists land 1945-6

KOREA

Yenan (Yan'an)

Nationalists Communists retake 1948

Chinan (Jinan) Sept. 1948

Lanchou (Lanzhou)

Sian (Xi'an) June 1948

Loyang (Luoyang) Apr. 1947

Yellow R.

Kaifeng June 1948

Hsuchou (Xuzhou) Jan. 1949

SICHUAN (occ. Dec. 1949)

Han R.

Begbu Jan. 1949

Huai R.

Nanking (Nanjing) April 1949

JAPAN

Chengdu (Chengtu) Dec. 1949

Yangtze R.

Wuhan May 1949

Shanghai May 1949

Chungking (Chongqing) Dec. 1949

Hangchou (Hangzhou) May 1949

Changsha Aug. 1949

Nanchang Oct. 1949

Kweiyang (Guiyang)

Autumn 1949

CHIANG Dec. 9 1949

TAIWAN

N

Canton (Guangzhou) Oct. 1949

HONG KONG (Br.)

Civil War battles, 1945–49

The battle lasted 65 days and broke the back of Chiang's military strength. In the same month of January 1949, Lin Biao took the isolated cities of Tianjin and then Beijing, whose general surrendered without a fight. His troops joined the Communists as did he.

By January 1949, it was clear that the Nationalists had lost, and Chiang resigned as President of China but retained the headship of the GMD. This simply complicated the chain of command and made the defence of southern China more difficult. There were some negotiations for peace, but the communist insistence on the punishment of war criminals, including Chiang in this category, ensured that the negotiations failed. The drive to the Yangtze was undertaken by communist armies now much more numerous than those still available to the GMD. Nanjing, Wuhan and Shanghai rapidly fell to communist forces in April and May 1949. Thereafter, Lin Biao pressed south to Canton, which fell in October, and then turned east to Xiamen, the embarkation point for retreating GMD armies heading for Taiwan. Here Chiang had decided to build a base, protected, he hoped, by the US fleet. After fierce fighting the port fell in November and only mopping-up operations in the west remained. In April, the communist forces showed their disdain for the imperialists of old, firing on the British frigate *Amethyst* and beating back naval forces sent up the Yangtze to help.

China had been united and was no longer going to suffer humiliation at the hands of foreigners. In Mao's famous words of 1949, 'The Chinese people have stood up.'

CONCLUSION

In accounting for the communist victory, many factors came into play. Chiang, already weakened by defeats during the war with Japan, made social and political blunders which undermined his rule still further. He appeared to want to resurrect his regime of the early 1930s with no real concessions to changing circumstances and pressures. The Democratic League had developed in the 1940s, seeking a third way between the Communists and Chiang. It drew its support from westernised liberals and intellectuals and wanted to see China develop as a democratic society. Chiang saw it as a challenge rather

KEY EVENT

The *Amethyst* incident (April 1949) The naval vessel was attempting to take supplies to the British Embassy in Nanjing and then evacuate civilians, when it came under communist fire and ran aground. Relief forces were beaten back, but it was eventually refloated and made it downstream to Shanghai.

than an opportunity to broaden his base. The GMD secret police were turned upon it and many who survived joined the Communists. Reference has already been made to his political mistakes in Manchuria, the appointment of outsiders and his failure to use the influence of the Young Marshal by releasing him and sending him north as governor. Chiang was a man of rigid and suspicious mind unwilling to compromise or change. Probably even more damaging to his support base was the **rampant inflation** that gripped the Chinese economy throughout these years. The ratio of the Chinese dollar to the US dollar fell from 7000:1 in January 1947 to 45,000:1 by August. Prices within China rocketed, bringing misery to millions. By April 1949, it has been calculated that a single grain of rice cost 2,500 Chinese dollars. Prices were 785,400,000 times greater than in 1937. This was particularly devastating in eroding the support of the urban middle classes who had been the bedrock of the regime.

The Communists appeared to enjoy a widening support base. Since Mao's rise to prominence, the party had targeted all classes other than the landlords and clients of foreign imperialists. It increasingly attracted intellectuals and liberals in the cities and was careful not to alienate the better-off peasants in the countryside. Its policy of rent control, aid to the village communities and **restrained and decent behaviour by its troops,** attracted the broad peasant masses. Its hold on the countryside was demonstrated in Manchuria and when Deng Xioaping was able to mobilise vast labouring armies to support the PLA in its 65-day battle at the end of 1948. It seemed to most thinking Chinese that by 1949, the Communists were the real heirs to the May 4th generation. They were the chosen instrument to regenerate China and lift it off its knees.

All the above contributed to the communist triumph, but it should not be forgotten that it was a military victory. Power, as Mao had famously said, came out of the barrel of a gun. The nature of the two armies partly explains the outcome. US observers during and after the war commented on the poor quality of many of Chiang's troops. Many were ill-trained, ill-fed and badly led.

KEY TERM

Rampant inflation had begun during the war. It arose from the continuous deficit the government faced. To solve the problem, the GMD simply printed money. The deficits got worse during the civil war and so did the printing of money. Food shortages and transport dislocation added to the price rises.

KEY TERM

Restrained and decent behaviour by Communist Party troops Since 1927, Mao and Zu De had stressed the need for soldiers to win the support of the peasantry and behave differently from the usual warlord troops. In Mao's Six Main Points for Attention (September 1927), his soldiers were told to pay for anything they damaged. Lin Biao later added Two Further Points – Don't molest Women and Dig latrines well away from homes. Such consideration, even if not always carried out, was a notable advance.

Corruption was endemic in the nationalist officer corps, with embezzlement of rations and false accounting of the real number of troops commonplace. The behaviour of many of the nationalist soldiers was reminiscent of the warlord era and the consequent alienation of the peasantry easy to understand. While not all the communist troops were perfect, and robbery and desertion did take place, all agree it was less common than in nationalist units. The Americans of the Dixie Mission in 1944 had been impressed with the energy and aggression of the communist troops, comparing them favourably with those of Chiang.

The Communists appear to have enjoyed superior intelligence gathering, i.e. they were better at infiltrating the GMD armies than vice versa. Chiang's assistant Chief of Staff, Liu Fei, was a communist spy as was the head of the GMD's War Planning Board. This gave the communist commanders an enormous advantage, knowing almost every move the Nationalists were about to make in advance. By comparison, the ruthless counter-intelligence operation of the Communists, run by Kang Sheng, seems to have rendered Chiang deaf and blind to communist planning. Perhaps most important was the quality of military leadership and strategic decision making. Chiang made a serious misjudgement in choosing to pour resources into Manchuria, far from his real bases of support. His later decision to fight it out at Xuzhou was a disaster. His whole attempt at micro-managing campaigns from a distance was mistaken and compared unfavourably with Mao's approach. Finally, in Lin Biao, the Communists appear to have had a general of outstanding ability.

The behaviour of the USA and the USSR are often raised in explaining the outcome. This is in reality a very subordinate consideration. Moscow, it is true, helped the Communists, initially in Manchuria, and armed them extensively with ex-Japanese weapons. This was less than the US$2 billion in aid provided by the USA to the Nationalists. The Soviets were often a handicap, ordering the Communists to leave the Manchurian cities in 1946 and even in 1949 advising the Reds not to cross the Yangtze. It is often asserted by critics of Truman that the USA could have done much more. US public opinion

TIMELINE

1945	Japanese surrender; Mao–Chiang talks
1945–47	Marshall mission
July 1946	Outbreak of civil war
1947	Communists abandon Yan'an
1948	Communist victory in Manchuria
January 1949	Beijing captured by Communists
April – May 1949	Capture of Shanghai and Nanjing
October 1949	Proclamation of People's Republic of China (PRC)

would not have countenanced direct military involvement. The USA refused a huge currency stabilisation loan in 1948 and the State Department vetoed an extra US$1.5 billion loan in 1949, proposed by some senators. To the US right, this was evidence of communist influence in the State Department. In reality, it was a result of a serious lack of trust in Chiang and the GMD regime. By October 1949, the USA did not intend even to defend Taiwan. The Korean War was to change this.

SUMMARY QUESTIONS

1 Why did the attempts to avoid a civil war in 1945–46 fail?

2 In what ways did the Nationalists contribute to their own defeat in the Civil War?

3 Why did the Communists achieve victory in 1949?

4 What role was played by the USA and USSR in determining the outcome of the Civil War?

CHAPTER 7

The new dynasty: China, 1949–56

INTRODUCTION

After 37 years of bloody chaos, China had a new emperor and a new dynasty. Mao proclaimed the People's Republic of China (PRC) on 1st October 1949. His high-pitched Hunanese-accented voice sounded out over Tiananmen Square from the Gate of Heavenly Peace. Victory had given him the Mandate of Heaven and the new dynasty clearly commanded widespread support. A large portrait of Mao hung from the walls and during the parade that followed the speech, crowds chanted 'Long live Chairman Mao'.

Over the next seven years, many of the aims of the May 4th generation were to be realised. Unity and national independence were to be established and consolidated. Foreigners were to be all but eliminated from Chinese soil and the country returned to a proud isolation. Drugs and bandits were to be largely removed by a determined brutality and women were to enjoy most of the freedoms espoused by the reformers of the early twentieth century.

THE GOVERNMENT OF THE PRC

Mao, like emperors before him, needed men to govern through, and instead of the gentry and mandarins there would be the Communist Party now 4.5 million strong. By the end of 1950, it would have 5.8 million members. They would provide the government of China with manpower at all levels. Nationally, the party was headed by the Central Committee of 44, itself headed by the **Politburo**. A five-man standing committee of the Politburo held supreme power, and consisted of Mao, **Liu Shaoqi**, Zhou Enlai, Zhu De and **Chen Yun**.

Parallel to the party was the governmental organisation it staffed. This was headed by Zhou Enlai as premier and Foreign Minister, positions he was to hold till 1976. Beneath him were 24 ministries. The third national

KEY TERM

Politburo was the policy committee of the party. Its name was taken from the similar body in the USSR; it held the same position as in the Soviet Union.

KEY PEOPLE

Liu Shaoqi (1898–1969) was second in importance to Mao and recognised as his likely successor until 1966. He was the leading expert on party organisation. Like Mao, he was of peasant origin from Hunan and worked easily with Mao in Yan'an. Unlike Mao, he was a much more restrained figure in personality and self projection. His neatly dressed grey figure contrasted with the sloppy bulk of the Chairman.

Chen Yun (1905–95) was one of the few Chinese Communists who was actually from the working class. He became the most important economic planner after 1949.

organisation was the PLA (People's Liberation Army), with Zhu De as the senior figure. These three organisations – party, government and army – intermeshed at all levels.

China was divided initially into six great regions and within each region four senior appointments were made: military commander of the PLA, government chairman, army political commissar and the key position, first party secretary. In Manchuria, in the North East Bureau, Gao Gong held all four posts. In the south west, Deng Xiaoping held the two crucial party posts of first secretary and political commissar. In the nationalist south, Lin Biao, the leading soldier of the regime, held three of the posts. The reality of these arrangements was that China was now unified and under a centralised control greater than ever before. In 1954, the country was reorganised into 21 provinces, five autonomous regions on the borders and two major urban centres (Shanghai and Beijing), but the grip of the party bureaucracy and the control from

China was divided into six regions. Each region was known as a bureau

Beijing remained as strong as ever. The scholar-bureaucrats were back in control, but the thought was now that of Marx as interpreted by Mao, not that of Confucius. The leading role of Mao's thought was even written into the Constitution of the PRC.

Mao's ultimate authority

There could be no doubt of Mao's ultimate authority. One man could clearly not govern in detail 500 million Chinese, but woe betide those who acted without his authority. In May 1953, he sent a sharp note to the party central bureaucracy:

> *Documents and telegrams sent out in the name of the Central Committee can be dispatched only after I have gone over them, otherwise they are invalid.*

It was Mao who ultimately set the pace and direction of change. He pushed for intervention in the Korean War, decided in 1952 that the bourgeoisie were no longer an ally of the proletariat and modulated the drive to collectivisation in agriculture, slowing or speeding it up. Mao thought of himself in terms of the first Qin Emperor who had unified China.

Mao's power in his own eyes is well illustrated, as is the concept of 'lost in translation', by the words he used to Edgar Snow in an interview in 1970. Mao used the first lines of a well-known classical couplet, describing himself as 'heshang dasan', literally a monk with an umbrella. The interpreter did not understand the classical allusion and Snow wrote of Mao as 'a poor monk wandering the world with a leaky umbrella'. This is not what the Chairman meant. The next two lines of the couplet, unspoken but assumed, gave Mao's real meaning – 'wufa wutian' – a man without law or god. There were no restraints on Mao.

Many of China's educated middle classes did not realise that the first Qin Emperor had returned. To many, 1949 represented the happy realisation of the hopes of the May 4th generation. Mao, himself was one of that generation. In 1940, he had written an essay, 'On the new democracy', and in 1949, this became the official

KEY EVENT

The **Chinese People's Political Consultative Conference** contained representatives of the Democratic League and other liberals who had abandoned Chiang and placed their faith in the Communist Party. The conference resolved on a programme of reform based on the original three principles of Sun Yat-sen: abolition of imperialist privileges, redistribution of land and friendship with the USSR. The meeting was largely window dressing for the regime and in no way marked an acceptance of parliamentary government. On this point, Mao agreed with his predecessors Chiang and Yuan Shikai.

description of the new regime and its policies. It was meant to unite workers, peasants and bourgeoisie in building a new China. Private property and private enterprise would be encouraged. Only landlords and agents of the Nationalist Party (GMD) regime and foreign interests were to be seen as enemies. Communism should not be seen as the enemy of freedom. The Communist Party convened a **Chinese People's Political Consultative Conference** to act as a provisional national assembly. Here was a promise of democracy, but slowly it became obvious that Mao drew his inspiration more from the Qin Emperor than western concepts of democracy and liberty.

PACIFICATION AND CONTROL

There was clearly a genuine need for increasing order and control. Thirty-seven years of warlords and war had produced social disintegration and criminal habits on a vast scale. Many men became bandits in the countryside. It has been estimated that there were as many as one million in 1949. Thieves and gangsters stalked the cities. Many women turned to prostitution as a means of survival. There were many ex-sympathisers with the GMD regime who had not escaped to Taiwan and sabotage expeditions were launched by the Nationalists from the safety of this hideaway, utilising supporters who had stayed behind. Some degree of repression in these circumstances was inevitable.

It was, however, carried out with a thoroughness worthy of the first Qin Emperor. The mood was intensified by the Korean war and the associated 'Resist America, Aid Korea' campaign. Around 28,000 suspected counter-revolutionaries were executed in Guangdong province alone. In the same area half a million rifles were confiscated. All people over 15 years of age needed official residence certificates from the police. Permission was needed to move. The basis of control became the danwei, a work or neighbourhood unit. It exercised surveillance over its members as well as serving other social, political or economic ends desired by the regime. It was the key building block in the creation of a totalitarian society. In contrast to the GMD regime, which relied simply on its secret police and spies, the communist regime went much further in demanding the active participation of all in surveillance. It is thought around 700,000 people throughout the country were executed or driven to suicide. Special labour camps were set up and rapidly filled with 1.5 million inmates. The Russian gulag was being replicated and remained a feature of Mao's regime. The first Qin Emperor would have approved.

Foreigners were particular objects of suspicion and the communist regime returned China to that closed world of the Qing Dynasty. The assets of foreign businesses were frozen and many were forced to sell out at cheap prices. Some had their businesses confiscated on the grounds of back taxes owed. An Italian and his Japanese neighbour in Beijing were accused of plotting to assassinate Mao and publicly shot. Five Canadian nuns in Canton were accused of murdering 2,000 Chinese babies. Huge protest rallies were whipped up in this way and by early 1951, most foreigners had reached the conclusion that it was better to leave than face popular attacks or state imprisonment for espionage.

The process of consolidating control was completed through two campaigns in 1951 and 1952. Firstly, the **Three Antis Campaign** targeted party members and bureaucrats and sought to combat corruption, waste and delay. Later, the **Five Antis Campaign** targeted businessmen with the aim of ending bribery, tax evasion, theft of state property, cheating and stealing economic information. Only one per cent of businessmen received prison sentences, but many more were given crippling fines or driven to suicide. The whole process was aimed at control and ending dissent. Terror and humiliation was meted out and the mass meeting became a way of life in most businesses. Positive attributes of the two campaigns were a reduction in criminal gang control in cities like Shanghai and a reduction in the endemic corruption of nationalist China. But the price was the subordination of the individual to the state in ways more total than that achieved in Nazi Germany.

Mass participation was also encouraged in a range of other state-sponsored organisations. Workers were encouraged to join trade unions, although their purpose was not workers rights but mass mobilisation in the

KEY EVENT

The **Three Antis Campaign** and the **Five Antis Campaign** were models for mass mobilisation in the cause of party power. Workers were encouraged to denounce their bosses in struggle meetings. Ritual humiliation and confession of the sort practised and perfected in the rectification campaigns in Yan'an in 1942–43 were now extended to all Chinese cities.

KEY TERM

Mass participation was one of the defining features of Chinese Communism in contrast to that of the USSR. Many of the atrocities committed in the Land Reform referred to below were not ordered or carried out by agents of the Beijing government but by ordinary villagers freed from restraint.

interests of the party. Likewise, the New Democratic Youth League had 9 million members by 1953. It later became the Communist Youth League (1957). The Women's Federation was set up and gained a membership of 76 million. The Communist Party claimed to be the agent of the masses and the masses were actively driven to be the agents of the party.

LAND REFORM

Land, and the ownership of land, was regarded by most Chinese people as probably the most vital of life's issues. It was intimately connected with survival or at the very least a satisfied belly. It was a complex question simplified by the Communist Party into a war on 'feudal' landlords and exploitation. The word 'feudal' imported from European thought had little meaning in most parts of China and certainly the patterns of land ownership bore little relationship to those of mediaeval Europe, which the word 'feudal' was meant to describe in Marxist jargon. In the north of China there were few landlords and only 10–15 per cent of farmers rented their land. In the south-west, in Sichuan, 56 per cent of people rented. Throughout the fertile lower Yangtze valley, wealthy peasants dominated food production and their surpluses fed the great cities. There was no agreed way on how to deal with the problem within the party. It had been one of the bones of contention between Mao and the returned Bolsheviks in the Jiangxi base area in the early 1930s. Mao had come to accept moderation as the best policy, allowing the richer peasants to flourish while targeting the larger land owners and village 'bullies'. In 1947, Liu Shaoqi had drafted a very egalitarian programme, closer to that of the returned Bolsheviks than that favoured by Mao. In 1948, Mao denounced Liu's scheme and in theory the party therefore remained committed to a modest redistribution. However, during the civil war, in the areas controlled by the Communists, more extreme redistribution schemes were pushed through in a bid to win the mass support of the poorer peasants. Old scores were paid off and this was often mixed with resentment of those who had collaborated with the Japanese.

When the party gained control of the whole of China in 1949, Land Reform was universally applied, but officially it was in moderate form. Mao in a report to the party in June 1950 stressed the need not to target the wealthy peasants, and the Agrarian Reform Law of that year adopted this moderate approach. In reality, there was a wide variation from place to place and as in so much of the new China, the initiative was left to the mobilised population. Villages were encouraged to hold 'struggle' meetings where rich landlords and 'village bullies' were denounced, beaten up and frequently executed.

Denunciation of a landlord during a 'struggle' meeting

In theory, they were to keep enough land to survive and their homes and any commercial property such as a mill, but the removal of the protection of the law opened the way to village anarchy and the repayment of old scores. It has been estimated that 40 per cent of the cultivated land was redistributed and that 60 per cent of the population benefited to varying degrees. The death toll was enormous but probably not as horrific as that engendered by Stalin's collectivisation drive in the early 1930s in Russia. One landlord family out of six had a member killed and the body count was probably somewhere between 750,000 and one million.

Land Reform was complete by 1952, and it had transformed China like nothing before. It had destroyed the old ruling elite and bought the support of vast numbers of peasants for the new regime. There were still real **inequalities in the villages** and tensions between poor peasants and their more wealthy neighbours. The winners in land reform had been the poor peasants and the owners of no land. The losers were clearly the gentry, who lost wealth, status and in many cases their lives.

KEY TERM

Inequalities in the villages
were in fact less than before. Before, the variation tended to be between approximately 0.4 hectares for poor peasants and 8 hectares for landlords. After, the variation was much narrower between the 0.8 hectares allocated to former landlords and the 1.5 hectares of a 'rich peasant'.

GENDER AND SOCIAL CHANGE

Women benefited from a **new marriage law** issued in 1950. Women were declared to have equal rights and arranged marriages were forbidden as were dowries and **concubinage.** Women's property rights were asserted as equal to men. Unmarried, divorced or widowed women could hold land in their own names. Children born out of wedlock were to have equal rights and divorce was to be available on equal terms, except that a man could not divorce his pregnant wife nor for a year after she had given birth. Such changes amounted to a social revolution and challenged many of the age-old traditions of Chinese family and village life.

War was also declared on prostitution. This involved mass participation and the danwei was crucial. All houses were registered and lists of visitors and their departure times kept by the street committees. The nosy neighbours would, in effect, destroy the trade. Known prostitutes and their pimps were sent to special re-education centres. The overall effect of this was to reduce the trade rapidly, and the new China had a somewhat puritanical air. The sexual behaviour of the leadership and Mao, in particular, hardly accorded with official policy.

Opium addiction was also targeted with some success. Poppy fields were uprooted and dealers shot. Addicts were simply killed or cured by withdrawal of the drug and thereafter their families made responsible for their good behaviour. The effectiveness of the Supression Policies varied widely from province to province.

COLLECTIVISATION OF AGRICULTURE

It had always been assumed that land reform would be only the first stage of a process that would build socialism in the countryside and release the resources in terms of food and labour for industrial growth. Larger units of production, it was argued, would be more efficient and produce more with less labour. On the other hand, the Chinese Communists were well aware of the disastrous collectivisation of agriculture in the USSR in the early 1930s and its unpopularity in the Jiengxi-Soviet. There had been massive resistance from the peasantry in the Soviet Union and production had actually fallen initially.

Until 1955, the Chinese Communist Party handled the problem sensibly. Mutual aid teams were encouraged in villages from 1951. These were usually composed of ten or fewer households, often of the same kinship group. In many ways, the arrangements formalised existing practises of cooperation between related families. Members pooled labour and equipment, particularly at key times of the year, like the harvest, but ownership of the land and its products remained private. By the end of 1952, 40 per cent of peasant households were team members.

The next stage was the encouragement of agricultural producers' cooperatives (APCs). These involved the central management of land but still under private ownership. Usually, three to five teams were involved, comprising 30 to 50 households. Members contributed their labour, animals and equipment and received a share in proportion to what was put in. The first of these was established in 1951, but none existed in south-east China before 1954. In other words, the pace of change varied enormously with much debate within the party as to the correct timescale. Richer peasants were tempted in by compensation paid in instalments for the use of their superior equipment or the greater number of their animals.

This was a far cry from the brutal expropriation of the kulaks (rich peasants) in Russia 20 years before. The drive for APCs became general in 1953. Some senior figures argued that it was pointless to push the process too far and too fast until there was the machinery available for cooperatives to buy. Mao urged the process forward, arguing that there had to be the cooperatives first as a market for machinery, but like others in the leadership he was sensitive to real peasant resistance. This tended to be marked where the local party tried to jump straight to APCs where there were no teams in place. In 1953, Mao reacted to increased resistance by condemning 'Rash Advance'. Unfortunately the ending of the push saw a growth in real rural capitalism with rich peasants hiring labour and buying land. This brought a condemnation of 'Rash Retreat.'

There was a fresh drive to push APCs. Resistance increased and some of the features that had marked Russian collectivisation began to appear. Rich peasants began to slaughter their animals rather than lose them to the APC. Severe flooding reduced the harvest and there were food riots. In the southern provinces the opposition to the Communists mounted considerably. Mao again called a halt in January 1955, by which time there were 670,000 APCs embracing one in seven households. Liu Shaoqi actually announced the disbandment of a quarter of them.

The key change came in April 1955, and it was orchestrated by the Chairman himself. It was a sign of things to come and perhaps marks Mao's abandoning of the practical approach to politics that had served him so well. In its place was to come the dogmatism he had denounced and a capacity for self-delusion. He visited the southern provinces to see for himself and talked extensively to local party officials who played down the resistance. Their self interest in terms of their power and status lay in pushing APCs. Mao was convinced to go on with the drive. As he admitted to party boss in charge, Deng Zihui, 'The peasants want freedom, but we want socialism.' They were ominous words and showed an awareness of the incompatibility of the two objectives. Mao called a **Conference of Local Party Secretaries in July 1955.** He pushed his vision of a socialist countryside to an audience who welcomed his instructions. The result was a frenetic drive for APCs. By January 1956, 80 per cent of households had been driven into cooperatives. Furthermore, what became known as higher level APCs now began to predominate. These comprised two to 300 households; there was no private ownership and no compensation for the pooling of assets. By the end of 1956, 88 per cent of peasants were members of advanced APCs and only 3 per cent still farmed as individuals. Land reform had also succeeded in achieving two of the other Party objectives, reducing the level of debts and installing Party cells at the grassroots of rural China. The new regime would in consequence exercise a degree of control far greater than that exercised by recent imperial dynasties. From the point of view of ideology, it was a triumph and Mao was ecstatic, but it marked a breach

KEY EVENT

The **Conference of Local Party Secretaries in July 1955** marked a vital change in Communist Party policy. Mao deliberately called the conference as a way of circumventing opposition within the Central Committee of the party. Having decided that the ending of private ownership was one of the most important developments in building his envisaged version of the new China, he was prepared to risk breaking the link he himself had so cherished between the party and the peasants.

with the millions of peasants whom the Communists had
been so successful in wooing. Economically, it was even
more of a mistake, but then economics had never been
one of Mao's strong points.

INDUSTRIALISATION AND THE FIRST FIVE-YEAR PLAN

China clearly intended to develop as a modern industrial
state. There was a long tradition of state-dominated
initiatives dating back to imperial China. Private
initiatives and liberal capitalism were more alien to the
Chinese historical tradition than the state dominated
model that the Communist Party chose to import from
the Soviet Union. The series of Five-Year Plans that had
been the hallmark of the Soviet economy since 1928 now
formed the pattern for economic development in China.
The Russian model of development was almost bound to
be adopted. The model actually seemed to work and it
was still possible to believe in it as a way forward for
humanity in the 1950s. Russia had defeated Nazi
Germany and seemed to have recovered from the war by
the death of Stalin, using the same centralised planning
that had marked development before the war. The
deficiencies of the Soviet model only really began to be
obvious from the 1960s and its truly disastrous nature
only in the 1980s and 1990s. By then, the Chinese, very
sensibly, had back-tracked and while still claiming to be
communist had adopted capitalism as a much more
efficient way of promoting economic growth.

This time also marked the closest period of cooperation
between the two fraternal socialist states. Soviet experts
poured into China to advise their Chinese comrades on
how to develop. As in the USSR, a balance sheet of
resources and objectives was drawn up. There was no
room for self-management or market forces. Planners not
consumers determined what was to be produced and, as
in Russia, the emphasis was on heavy industry, steel coal
and electric power. It was all to be paid for by the
peasants, hence the need to increase control of agriculture
through the promotion of collective farming. Peasants
were forced to sell a substantial portion of their grain to
the state at low prices. This could be used to feed the
growing work force in the cities.

A new currency was introduced, the renminbi, and the communist government did not make the mistake of overprinting money. In fact, with the ending of the Korean war it was able to cut spending in most fields including even health and welfare. Ministries multiplied to control the process of industrialisation: coal, electric power, agriculture and petroleum in 1955, and another nine were added in 1956. However, in contrast to the GMD regime, corruption was kept to a minimum as were the rewards paid to the burgeoning civil service. It was enough to be fed and housed and to serve the new China.

The plan ran from 1953 to 1957 and seems to have been an extraordinary success. There was undoubtedly a fund of good will, considerable spare capacity and, most importantly, the opportunities provided by a potentially rich land with an intelligent, hard working people. Peace and order after 37 years of chaos were probably the most important ingredients of the plan's triumph. Coal production virtually doubled and electric power nearly tripled. Steel production quadrupled. There were more ships and locomotives and a staggering increase in the number of bicycles manufactured. Here were the first steps on the road to industrial transformation.

CONCLUSION

Much had been achieved by the new dynasty and its emperor in a mere seven years. Few human societies had been so purposefully transformed in such a short time. The restoration of order, unity and stability was probably the greatest gain for most Chinese citizens, assuming they were not one of the many corpses, or related to one of the many corpses, that the process had entailed. Bandits, gangsters, drug dealers, pimps and prostitutes had all been seriously reduced in numbers.

The central government in Beijing had a grip on the provinces and on the individual citizen, never seen before. Family life and village life had been transformed by the new Marriage Law and Land Reform and then transformed again by the introduction of collectivisation. Foreign businessmen had been forced out and Chinese-run businesses forced into partnership with the state or wholly taken over. The old elites, whether gentry in the countryside or **the bourgeoisie in the cities had been destroyed**, and in their place a new elite, the party cadres now ruled. New business ventures had been started, promising modernity and a catching up with the hated foreign devils who had tormented China for so long. Hundreds of thousands, if not millions, had died in these years and even more entered labour camps, but it really did seem that the Chinese people had stood up.

SUMMARY QUESTIONS

1 In what ways did the Communist Party consolidate its grip on power in the two years after October 1949?

2 Why was the Communist Party able to transform agriculture and village life in the years 1949–56?

3 Why was a Five-Year Plan introduced in 1953?

4 'A social, political and economic revolution!' Is this an appropriate description of developments in China in the years 1949–56?

TIMELINE

1949	Proclamation of PRC
1950	Agrarian Reform Law; Marriage Law
1951	Three Antis Campaign
1952	Five Antis Campaign
1953	Five-Year Plan for industrial development started
1955–6	Drive for collectivisation

CHAPTER 8

Politics, personalities, dissent and repression: China,1954–58

INTRODUCTION

The new communist regime had come to power in 1949 with the expressed intention of transforming the country. It called itself the 'People's Republic' and the army was the 'People's Liberation Army (PLA).' These titles implied some element of greater democracy and personal liberty. Many of the intelligentsia, who were not Communists, supported the new government and some returned from exile to take part in building a new China. They hoped to see more popular participation and more respect for individual rights. They were to be disappointed.

THE BURDEN OF CHINA'S PAST AND HOPES FOR THE FUTURE

China had never been a **democracy** in the sense that Britain, the USA or even France had in the nineteenth century. The French tradition of democracy is essentially different from the Anglo-Saxon one of Britain and the USA. The Anglo-Saxon tradition accepts the notion of many interests within a society and it is the task of government to reconcile these peacefully within a framework of law. The French tradition owes much to Jean Jacques Rousseau and his idea of the 'general will'. This assumes that society has a set of common interests deep down, which it is the task of government to articulate and put into practice. In so far as communist China accepted a notion of democracy, it was the French version and it is no accident that Zhou Enlai and Deng Xiaoping had both been students in France. Rousseau's ideas can of course justify a totalitarian regime in which the government, claiming to act for the 'people', abuses the rights of individuals or minorities.

There was no Chinese tradition of popular participation in government through legislative bodies at either provincial or national level. There was no liberal tradition of personal freedom and individual rights *vis à vis* the

---

KEY TERM

Democracy literally means rule by the people, and in the modern world has come to be equated with some system of fair and free elections when the government is chosen by the majority or the largest minority. The key idea is the ability of the electorate to change the government peacefully by the exercise of a vote.

In many people's minds, democracy and the **liberal tradition of personal freedom and individual rights** are treated as one and the same, which they are not. It is quite possible to have democracy but not liberty, i.e. the majority might choose the government, which then persecutes a minority as in Nazi Germany.

state. The state had a monopoly of violence, which it used in various brutal ways to force the individual to conform.

Under western influence, there had been a growing demand among the educated for both greater individual liberty and more popular participation. Such developments had begun in the last years of the Qing Dynasty and the revolution of 1912 had brought high hopes among the students and intelligentsia that China could be transformed. These hopes were most noisily voiced by the May 4th generation and embodied in the Three Principles of Sun Yat-sen's Nationalist Party. National

A traditional Chinese slow execution

unity and defeat of imperialist influences had also been an equal objective and under both Chiang and Mao this had been given greater priority. Improving living standards had also been one of Sun Yat-sen's principles and, in all fairness, this probably mattered to most Chinese men and women more than the other two. To Mao and the Communist Party, this too had greater priority over the issue of democracy, and individual rights were not on the agenda at all. They were associated with an alien west, now firmly excluded from Chinese life.

Confucian thought had never emphasised the individual but had concerned itself primarily with social harmony, stressing obedience to legitimate authority. There was no notion of the important western concept of what has been termed 'generic individualism,' i.e. each person is interchangeable and shares universal rights. In China, the tradition was one of service according to individual position. The mandarin governed and could speak at court; the peasant produced food. Each individual was to contribute to the greater good of 'all under heaven' – the Chinese state. Individuals were thus unimportant and insignificant except for their contribution to the whole. The individual merchant had always been a suspect figure and economic activity was carefully regulated and even dominated by the state. It was probably no accident that the western system of thought that was actually embraced was **Marxism,** as interpreted by the Soviet state.

Marxism and the Chinese Communist Party

Like Confucianism, Marxist-Leninism, to give Soviet Marxism its correct name, stressed the role of the group. Class conflict was the all-important engine driving human society. Individuals were of little consequence as either victims or determinants of outcome. Lenin had happily ordered the massacre and extermination of priests, bourgeois or any wrong thinking individual who stood in the way of the triumph of the proletariat. In the first year alone of Bolshevik rule in Russia, 6,000 people had been executed for political offences, more than in the whole reign of the Tsar since 1894. As time went on, thousands were to become millions under Stalin. The Chinese Communist Party (CCP) had imbibed this approach and although Mao had adjusted Marxism in many ways to meet the needs and peculiarities of Chinese society, a greater concern for individual rights was not one of these adjustments.

Mao and the other leading members of the CCP created an official ideology, which claimed to be Marxist but in reality was an amalgam of traditional Chinese thought, with its emphasis on the greater good of the state and Marxist–Leninism. Mao himself expressed great sympathy for the first Qin Emperor and his belief in **Legalism.** Likewise, he retained a regard for Stalin as a creative ruler and any reservations he might have had about the Russian dictator were not to do with Stalin's lack of respect for human rights. Stalin, for his part, doubted if Mao could really be considered a Marxist. Mao used some of the jargon of Marxism and thought of himself as a Marxist thinker, but his emphasis on the peasantry as a revolutionary force rather than the urban working class and his genuine belief in mass mobilisation as a solution to problems meant that at the very least his emphasis was different from that of Russian Marxism. As Mao himself famously put it in 1956:

We must not blindly follow the Soviet Union ... Every fart has some kind of smell, and we cannot say that all Soviet farts smell sweet.

Mao's belief in 'human will' was even more important in dividing him from orthodox Marxist thought. Marxists of all shades pride themselves on scientific analysis. They claim 'objectivity'. Mao, like Hitler, believed in the triumph of the human will over objective reality. He was fond of the story of the old man and the mountain who argued that if he and his descendants dug long enough they would remove a mountain obstruction. All that was necessary was to persist and will the desired end. Will combined with mass mobilisation could achieve anything, according to Mao. This approach caused concern to his more orthodox Marxist colleagues such as Liu Shaoqi. Mao, again like Hitler, was a romantic and an artist. He wrote rather fine poems in classical Chinese. He viewed himself not simply as the instrument of the blind impersonal forces beloved of Marxist thinkers but as a creative explosive force able to write on the blank page of human history. He saw himself almost as **Nietzche's Superman**, rising above the world of ordinary mortals to shape the destiny of mankind. He was more an existentialist than a Marxist. He was without law or god.

Yet in practical, political terms Mao was a formidable, subtle player. He was adept at recognising contradictions and valid conflicting positions and playing one position off against another, shifting from one side to another according to circumstances. Now he would hasten the move to collectivised farming; now argue that the pace was too fast. Now argue for closer collaboration with Russia; now urge distance, always using the earthy language of his peasant origins. There was also an iron will and courage. He hated being controlled even for his own safety and resented the party apparatus' attempts to regulate his life. In 1956, Mao decided that he wished to swim in China's greatest river, the Yangtze. It had an incredible fast current, deadly whirlpools and sections heavily infested with disease-carrying snails. When the head of his security told him it was too dangerous he was told 'Gun dan' which, loosely translated, means 'Get your balls out of here'. Mao got his way and floated for two hours down the flooded Yangtze for over 15 miles. Even

KEY TERM

Nietzche's Superman
F W Nietzsche (1844–1900) was a very influential German thinker who stressed the importance of will and human creativity. In one of his most famous books, *Thus Spake Zarathustra,* he proclaimed the coming of the *Übermensch* or over man, usually translated as superman.

more, he hated the party's attempts to control and regulate his political initiatives. The three ruling bodies – party, PLA and the bureaucracy – all were viewed with suspicion by the new emperor, who in the last resort was determined to get his way.

THE PEOPLE'S LIBERATION ARMY

In 1950, the PLA was 5 million strong. It had enabled the Communist Party to seize power in China and then gone on to administer a bloody nose to the Americans in Korea (see Chapter 11). It was a glorious and key part of the People's Republic. But it had to change. As a peace-time force it would be slimmed down. The crippling burden of military expenditure had been one of the great weaknesses of the Nationalist Party (GMD) regime of Chiang Kaishek. The Korean war had also revealed serious short-comings. Enthusiasm and courage were not enough. Mao had expressed the problem in his usual elliptical way. Strategically, the Americans were a paper tiger, but tactically they were a real tiger. They could bite and they had. **Peng Dehuai**, the commander in the Korean war and then appointed Minister of Defence, saw the need for modernisation. China needed a smaller but more technologically proficient force.

The numbers were gradually reduced. By 1953, it was 3.5 million. Three million soldiers had been demobilised and 1.5 million new conscripts called up. By 1957, it was 2.5 million. Even so, it was still the largest army in the world and every year 800,000 men were conscripted for three years' service. Expenditure was not cut but allowed to stabilise, falling as a percentage of government expenditure as national income rose under the first Five-Year Plan. Money was spent on shaping a more technically advanced force. Engineering and signalling corps were created and an airforce equipped with Russian MIGs manufactured under licence in Manchuria. Promising officers were sent to the Soviet Red Army's staff college in Kiev and new officer training academies were set up in Beijing and Nanjing. China even began to develop her own rockets and ballistic missiles in 1955. A Chinese nuclear programme was also begun with Soviet assistance.

These changes all meant that the essential nature of the PLA changed, as it became more professional. Much of its old egalitarianism began to disappear. Fourteen precise ranks were instigated in 1955 with sharply differentiated pay scales. Colonels received 30 times the pay of a private. The old links with the civilian population so carefully fostered during the civil war began to break down. The PLA began to resemble the army of Chiang Kaishek or even the old banner armies of the Qing. There were numerous examples of abuse of the civilian population and in particular of women.

Mao, while anxious to have the great power status that only a modern army could bring, was equally determined to maintain control and prevent the emergence of rival power bases or worst of all see a return to the regional warlordism of the 1920s. Mao had enunciated his famous doctrine on the role of the army in 1938:

> *Every communist must grasp this truth, 'Political power grows out of the barrel of a gun'. Our principle is that the Party commands the gun, and the gun must never be allowed to command the Party.*

The original six vast regions established in 1949 were abolished in 1954 and replaced by 13 new regions usually comprising two provinces. This was remarkably like the old imperial system. The regions were answerable to a military affairs commission, chaired by Mao, and the ministry of defence, under Peng Dehuai. Conscripts were subjected to a barrage of propaganda from the party and the army remained a crucial instrument of spreading the party's message throughout rural China. A new code of behaviour for the PLA was drawn up by its political department in 1956, stressing the need for close cooperation with collective farms, even down to units making their excrement available as fertiliser. Power might come out of the barrel of a gun, but the party and, more particularly, Mao would control it.

THE PARTY AND THE BUREAUCRACY

Mao was sensitive to challenges of all types and one of the most mysterious episodes in the early life of the republic was the so-called plot and purge of **Gao Gang** and

KEY PERSON

Gao Gang (1905–54) had established a communist base area in Shaanxi in the early 1930s and it was to this that the Long Marchers had come in 1935. In Yan'an he had worked closely with Mao and in 1949 was rewarded with the important region of Manchuria which contained most of China's heavy industry. Much to do with his downfall is still shrouded in mystery.

Rao Shushi in 1954. Gao Gang had built up a powerful regional base in Manchuria and closely modelled the power structure there on that of Stalinist Russia. He was very much at the forefront of those urging a slavish copying of the Soviet path to growth and development with an emphasis on heavy industry. In 1952, he became head of the state planning commission and as such the most important figure in the Five-Year Plan. Mao was increasingly talking of giving up the role of head of state, which bored him and the acknowledged successor was Liu Shaoqi. Gao began plotting to replace Liu and established an alliance with the regional boss of Shanghai, Rao Shushi. Mao was alerted by Deng Xiaoping and Chen Yun. The latter had spent much time in Moscow during the 1930s watching Stalin at work and knew the golden rule that only the boss was allowed to plot. In China, this meant Mao. Mao allowed things to develop, possibly encouraging Gao in 1953 before denouncing him at a Politburo meeting on 24 December. Both Gao and Rao were destroyed. Mao referred to Gao as a sinister wind. Gao committed suicide in 1954 and Rao was imprisoned where he died 20 years later. The emperor had struck. It served as a warning to others, not to take the initiative and to try to build too strong a regional base and not to follow too slavishly the Soviet model. Perhaps it was also designed as a warning to Liu and Zhou Enlai who were the chief intended victims of the plot to remember how much they needed Mao.

Mao was irritated by the opposition from Zhou and the party bureaucracy to his schemes for pushing ahead faster to socialism and collectivisation in 1955. He was concerned as he had been with the army that old habits were returning, and he blamed the **revolts in eastern Europe in 1956** on creeping bureaucratism which had divided the Communist Parties in those countries from the people. Mao warned in a speech in 1956:

> *The Communist Party has to learn its lesson. We must be vigilant, and must not allow a bureaucratic work-style to develop. We must not form an aristocracy divorced from the people.*

Mao was aware that the party cadres were increasingly behaving as the scholar-bureaucrats of imperial China.

KEY EVENTS

Revolts in eastern Europe in 1956 Following the famous destalinisation speech by Khrushchev in February, discontent simmered in eastern Europe, where communist regimes had been brutally enforced in the wake of the advancing Soviet armies in 1945. There were demonstrations in Poland in June and the Polish Communists turned to a recently released 'liberal' Communist, Gomulka. He was cleverly able to persuade the Russians to accept modest changes. In Hungary, there was no such peaceful change. Widespread popular revolt and attacks on the secret police were eventually crushed by Soviet tanks in November.

Their position was almost symbolised by Zhou Enlai, with his impeccable manners and beautifully cut suits. Mao was often inclined to refer to Zhou's Confucian tendencies. If Mao was unhappy at the PLA turning increasingly into something resembling the old imperial army and the party and the **bureaucracy** developing into mandarins, he was not apparently aware of his own transformation into an emperor or if he was, he saw nothing wrong with it.

Mao's unhappiness with some of the party's leaders was increased by the events at the party's eighth Congress held in September 1956. Earlier in the year, in February, Nikita Khrushchev, the new Soviet leader, had denounced the dead Stalin and the cult of personality. Deng Xiaoping and Zhu De had been delegates to the Congress and heard for themselves Khrushchev's shattering message. It was perhaps inevitable in consequence that there would be some down playing of Mao's role in China and a new emphasis on collective leadership.

In the event, the new party constitution removed references to the Thought of Mao Zedong as the guiding ideology of the party. Most of the arrangements for the Congress and the chief speeches were given by Liu Shaoqi and Deng Xiaoping. Mao gave a brief introductory speech. He later complained that he had not seen the new draft constitution or the official report delivered by Liu to the Congress. Apparently, it had been sent to him in the early hours when he usually worked, but on this occasion he had taken a sleeping pill and never read it. This was to be the cause of much trouble between Mao and the party leadership. In the words of **Mao's doctor**:

> *They viewed Mao as the first amongst equals. Mao's view, however, was more imperial. He saw himself and his will as supreme and resented any indication to the contrary.*

THE HUNDRED FLOWERS CAMPAIGN, 1957

The origins of this movement in the spring of 1957 is complicated and still subject to much debate. Various issues came together to produce it. There was real tension between the intellectual elite and the Communist Party. The educated tended to come from the wealthier classes

KEY TERM

Bureaucracy There had been a massive expansion from about 720,000 state officials in 1949 to 7.9 million in 1958. There had never been such a degree of government control in China.

KEY PERSON

Mao's doctor, Doctor Zhisui Li, was Mao's personal physician from 1954 to 1976. In 1988, he emigrated to the USA and wrote his memoirs, which were published in 1994 as *The Private Life of Chairman Mao.*

KEY TERM

The Hundred Flowers is an old adage referring back to the period before the unification of China under the Qin Emperor when different philosophies, most notably Confucianism and Legalism, were in contention. In May 1956, Lu Dingyi made reference to it in a Party debate – 'Let a hundred flowers bloom, and a hundred schools of thought contend'.

Lao She (1899–1966) was the author of the celebrated satirical novel, *Cat Country* in 1932 and the best seller *Rickshaw*.

and many had had connections with the GMD regime or had been educated abroad. Despite such potential antagonisms, most of the intelligentsia had not left in 1949–50 and in fact many had actually returned from self-imposed exile to contribute to the new China. China's most famous author, **Lao She**, had returned from the USA in 1950. The new China subjected its intellectuals to endless bouts of self-criticism and re-education. All had to write self-critical autobiographies denouncing their past life and incorrect thoughts. Yet the new China needed the educated as the Five-Year Plans made clear. Scientists complained of ideology stifling research and hampering access to western research papers and Zhou Enlai and others came to see the need for a freer climate which would aid economic growth. How much freedom should be allowed was a moot point. In 1955, the respected author and editor, Hu Feng, who was also a party member, attacked the idea that all literature should serve political ends and had the temerity to suggest that Marxism could stifle creativity. This was going too far and after bitter denunciation and the rejection of three pieces of self-criticism as inadequate, he was imprisoned. Nevertheless, the feeling continued to grow that there should be some degree of liberalisation, and Mao himself appears to have increasingly accepted this. In the autumn of 1956, Wang Meng, the 22-year old son of a professor of philosophy at Beijing, published a short novel, *The Young Man Who Has Just Arrived at the Organisation Department*. It attacked laziness and incompetence in the communist bureaucracy.

'On the correct handling of contradictions amongst the People' During the speech, Mao used the slogan about letting a hundred flowers bloom and argued that it was impossible to grow only fragrant flowers and not poisonous weeds:

What is there to fear from the growth of fragrant flowers and poisonous weeds? There is nothing to fear.

It coincided with concerns arising from the rebellion in Hungary and Mao's own growing worries about the party and bureaucracy. Mao increasingly felt he could use the intellectuals to shake up the party. He would unleash a tide of energy which would reinvigorate the country and damage those who had had the temerity to frustrate the Chairman's will. In February 1957, he delivered a speech, **'On the correct handling of contradictions amongst the People'**. In it, he argued that contradictions were inevitable even under socialism and as long as these were not antagonistic, i.e. class-based, then it was natural and good to let them be aired. Holding them in caused explosions like that in Hungary. As he typically expressed it on another occasion:

> *If they have something to fart about, let them fart! If it's out, then one can decide whether it smells bad or good. If the people think their farts stink, they will be isolated.*

It took time to get the movement going. The example of Hu Feng was fresh in many of the intelligensia's minds and the party bureaucrats were clearly reluctant to act. *The People's Daily* was very slow in encouraging the movement. Mao called in the editor and made it clear that he must support the movement. From April, Mao was able to prod the movement into life. On 13th April, *The People's Daily* had an editorial encouraging the movement, and papers across the country followed suit. The criticisms began and at first were often trivial, but by early May the torrent had been unleashed and it took Mao by surprise. The rule of the party itself was now attacked and there was a demand for genuine democracy. Even Mao himself was likened to the head of a monastery who dictated the scriptures. From 15th May, he began to change tack and suggest that the movement be controlled. On 8th June, *The People's Daily* suggested that a small number were abusing the movement and suggested a counter-attack. Mao's speech of February was published on 19th June but with important changes inserted. Now it was made clear that criticisms must unite not divide and must buttress the Communist Party's hold on power. What followed was a crackdown.

Most commentators tend to take the view of his doctor, Li Zhisui in his memoirs, *The Private Life of Chairman Mao* (1994):

> *Mao knew the intellectuals felt betrayed. 'Now some of the rightists are saying that I plotted against them,' he said after the June 19 version of the speech was published. 'They say that I urged them to participate in the blooming-and-contending campaign and then retaliated when they did as I said. But I haven't hatched any "secret plot". I did it openly. I told the rightists to criticize us in order to help the party. I never asked them to oppose the party or to try to seize power from the party. I told them from the very beginning not to make trouble. "It won't be*

good for you to make trouble," I warned them. "Just try to be helpful to the Communist Party." Some of them listened. But most of them didn't. Mao, I know now, was being disingenuous. His strategy of using the intellectuals to criticise his foes within the party had backfired.

Jung Chang in her recent biography of Mao, *Mao: The Untold Story* (2005), takes a different line:

But with the trend in the Communist world blowing towards de-Stalinisation, Mao decided it was not wise to be too blatant about launching a purge. To create a justification, he cooked up a devious plan ... Few guessed that Mao was setting a trap, and that he was inviting people to speak out so that he could then use what they said as an excuse to victimise them. Mao's targets were intellectuals and the educated, the people most likely to speak up.

Philip Short in his biography, *Mao: A Life of Mao* (1999), takes essentially Doctor Li's approach:

The 'Hundred Flowers' was the most ambitious attempt ever undertaken in any communist country to combine a totalitarian system with democratic checks and balances. Even Mao was unsure what it would produce. 'Let's try it and see what it's like,' he said at one point ...

Why then did he decide that a crackdown was necessary?

There is no simple answer. The 'Hundred Flowers' was not, as Mao's victims and supporters both claimed, a carefully contrived trap from the start, an example of the Chairman's cunning in 'luring the snake out of its hole'.

Whatever the original motives, there can be no argument about the results, a thorough going purge of the intelligentsia.

THE ANTI-RIGHTIST CAMPAIGN

The clampdown on those members of the intelligentsia denounced as 'rightists' exceeded anything so far meted out to intellectuals. All of suspect class origins were targeted. There tended to be a quota system as in the Russian purges. There was a widespread perception in local party hierarchies that 5–10 per cent were rightists and there tended to be a search to come up with the appropriate number. Anyone with a suspect past was likely to be denounced and prosecuted. Those educated abroad, or of landlord origins or associated indirectly with the GMD regime were likely to be indicted. Somewhere between 300,000 and 500,000 people were persecuted and sent to labour camps for correction. The numbers actually killed were small, but the suffering was great. Wang Meng, whose book attacking bureaucratic corruption had been looked upon with favour in 1956 was sentenced to five years' hard labour in a rural area. He was released early in 1961 but later exiled to the far west. The most eminent female novelist, Ding Ling, who had joined the Party in 1932 and won the Stalin prize for her novel of 1951, praising collectivisation, was exiled to northern China and spent the next 20 years either in exile or labour camps. One of the most moving accounts of a young intellectual who suffered at this time has been translated and published in the west as *Grass Soup*. Those labelled rightists and their families were ruined. To escape a shared fate, wives divorced husbands and vice versa.

CONCLUSION

Terror and discipline imposed a deadening hand over the new China that had been greeted with so much enthusiasm in 1949.

The old China of the pre-Qing imperial dynasties had once again reasserted itself, extinguishing the hopes of greater personal freedom and a genuine voicing of dissent. The spring of blooming flowers had been very short. Winter returned. The chill struck deep and lasted long.

An anti-rightist rally denounces Zhang Bojun

TIMELINE

1954	Fall of Gao Gang
1955	Persecution of Hu Feng
1956	Eighth Party Congress
February –April 1957	Launching of Hundred Flowers campaign
June 1957	Ending of Hundred Flowers
July 1957 onwards	Anti-rightist campaign

SUMMARY QUESTIONS

1 In what ways might Mao be considered as not an orthodox Marxist thinker?

2 In what ways did the PLA change in the years 1950–57?

3 Why was the Hundred Flowers campaign introduced in 1957?

4 To what extent does China deserve to be described as a totalitarian state in the years 1954–57?

CHAPTER 9

The Great Leap Forward

INTRODUCTION

The Great Leap Forward was launched formally in May 1958 at the second session of the Eighth Party Congress. As in the first session, Liu Shaoqi made the principal report, but this time it was not the sober controlled speech of 1956 but a rallying cry to create a new China almost overnight. Mao had spoken only briefly at the first session; now he spoke five times, plainly excited by the drama about to be unleashed on his 600 to 700 million subjects. The aim was to transform China in record time, a dash for economic growth and development. The twin slogans were **'Politics in charge'** and **'Walking on two legs'**. China would overtake Britain as an economic power in less than 15 years it was announced. Life for most Chinese would be transformed for the better with every need catered for. All that was necessary was enthusiasm and real hard work. Mass mobilisation could solve anything. The reality was somewhat different. Heaven did not emerge but something akin to hell. Large numbers of ordinary Chinese men and women died because of the misplaced and almost mad enthusiasm of their emperor. The story is a classic warning against a political system which lacks checks and balances on its government's actions.

ORIGINS OF THE GREAT LEAP

The change grew out of the complex interaction of several factors. Mao was the undoubted driving force behind the policy. It appealed to his fundamental political beliefs and prejudices. He had a faith in willpower to overcome almost any obstacles and in the power of the mobilised masses to achieve anything. All that was necessary was to release the energies of the people. He disliked experts and the Hundred Flowers campaign had added to his dislike. The people, however, could be moulded to his and the party's will. He expressed this view in an extreme form in an article of April 1958:

*China's 600 million people have two remarkable
peculiarities; they are, first of all, poor, and secondly,
blank. That may seem like a bad thing, but it is really a
good thing. Poor people want change, want to do things,
want revolution. A clean sheet of paper has no blotches,
and so the newest and most beautiful words can be written
on it, the newest and most beautiful pictures can be
painted on it.*

Mao's self-confidence, never in short supply, had grown to
new heights with the easy success of the move to
collectivisation in 1956 and the ease with which the
bourgeoisie had been destroyed. This, often called the
Little Leap, had been opposed by the more cautious of the
bureaucrats, headed by Zhou Enlai. It seemed to Mao that
he had once again been proved right and Zhou, as so
often in the past, wrong. Zhou, not for the first time and
not for the last, had to confess his errors and mistaken
judgement. The anti-rightist campaign, in full flow since
the autumn of 1957, intimidated Zhou and many of his
supporters in the government.

There were, in addition, very real practical difficulties in
the way of continuing with the techniques used in the
first Five-Year Plan. There was a real shortage of experts
and despite the presence of many Russian helpers and
advisers, this did not solve the problem. Furthermore,
dependence on another country was humiliating even if
the dependence was on a fraternal ally like the Soviet
Union. Chinese xenophobia was strong and just as Chiang
Kaishek had resented US patronage, many Communists
from Mao downwards resented being patronised by
Russians.

Furthermore, the basic premise of the Soviet model of
development did not seem to operate in China. The
assumption behind the Stalinist Plans of the 1930s, and
copied by Chinese planners, was that agriculture would
generate the wealth to pay for industrialisation. More
food could be extracted from the collectives to feed the
growing urban workforce and to export to pay for heavy
capital imports. This was not happening. Industrial
production under the first plan had soared, but
agricultural production had stagnated. In 1957, food

production had increased by only 1 per cent, while the population had increased by 2 per cent. Most of the countryside's production was being used up in the country. The only alternative was to go further down the Soviet path with draconian food procurement such as had been used **in 1932 in the USSR**. This had produced rural misery and famine. The Chinese Communist Party, unlike that of the USSR, was dominated by rural membership and such a policy would not be acceptable. More Soviet development loans were not an option either. What could be spared in the way of Soviet aid was going to eastern Europe to try to prevent further popular risings, like those in Hungary and Poland.

The answer had to come from within China and be a specifically Chinese solution. Mao and others in the Politburo hit upon the idea of decentralising control and letting enlarged agricultural units generate both more food and industrial products, hence the slogan 'Walking on two legs'. The emergence of these larger agricultural units was almost coincidental. In the winter of 1957–58, the party had promoted a series of gigantic irrigation and water control projects. Around 100 million peasants had been mobilised in various areas and this involved close cooperation between several collectives. The idea was born of the super-collective, which Mao named **people's communes**. These would be the instruments for the Great Leap Forward.

The opposition to the new approach was minimal. In addition, Liu Shaoqi was happy to embrace a scheme which heightened his importance at the expense of his chief political rival, Zhou. In February, general oversight of economic development was transferred from the state bureaucracy under premier Zhou to the party organisation under Liu and Deng Xiaoping. A new tier of party officials was put in place to manage the new communes and push them forward. Self-interest and increased self importance pushed many in the party into support.

Furthermore, there was a new spirit of optimism abroad, much of it coming from Moscow. **'The East Wind was prevailing over the West wind.'** Perhaps, this was the last time that it really was possible to believe that

KEY EVENT

In 1932, in the USSR the interlinked drive for collectivisation and industrialisation had produced a horrendous famine in the Ukraine and some neighbouring areas. Five to seven million people died largely as a result of government policies.

KEY TERM

People's communes Mao chose the name, which had been used to describe the great popular revolt in Paris in 1871.

'The East wind was prevailing over the West wind' comes from Mao's favourite novel, the eighteenth-century Chinese classic, *Dream of the Red Chamber*.

Communism was essentially superior to capitalism. Khrushchev exuded a bumptious self-confidence. He really believed that socialism was going to deliver a superior social and economic system. It is touching now to read of his belief that the superior height of Russian jet airliners reflected the superiority of Soviet technology when in reality it reflected the inferiority of Soviet airstrips. None could, however, deny the Soviet achievement of launching the first satellite into space in October 1957 and then in November launching a dog into space. Soviet technology seemed to have stolen a march on the capitalist west. Mao attended the anniversary celebrations of the Russian revolution and was carried away by the euphoria. The Russians boasted that in 15 years they would overtake the USA in the production of steel and coal and other industrial commodities. Mao, not to be outdone, claimed that China would overtake Britain.

Over the next few months the self-confidence grew, and Mao's belief in the possibilities of almost unlimited growth was infectious. Mao embarked on a fact-finding mission throughout his empire. He found what he wanted to find – limitless possibilities. By May 1958, he believed it would be possible to overtake Britain in seven years. Steel production estimates were raised and raised again. Eventually, he announced that by the 1970s China would be producing several times the entire world production. Grain production estimates were subject to the same fantastic inflationary predictions. China as a whole was about to enter the madhouse and nobody could tell the chief lunatic he was imagining things.

The Four No's campaign

A taste of what was to come (and what was wrong), came about in October 1957 at a full meeting of the Central Committee of the Party when Mao announced the extermination of the Four Pests. It led to the Four No's campaign: no rats, no sparrows, no flies and no mosquitoes. The impact on rats was not notable, but the sparrows died in their millions. Mao had decided that they ate the grain and food production would be boosted if sparrows were no more. All over China, the word went out to kill sparrows. Men, women and children worked with a vengeance, beating gongs, screaming at sparrows and pursuing them with bamboo poles. They were not allowed to alight anywhere without being chivvied back into flight so that they eventually collapsed of exhaustion. Cart loads of dead and dying birds were to be seen. Here was mass mobilisation at work. When a plague of caterpillars emerged in 1958 attacking plants and crops, sparrows were dropped from the death list – sparrows eat caterpillars. They were replaced by bed bugs. Flies and mosquitoes also suffered persecution but with no long-term effect. In the short term, individuals enjoying the privacy of the lavatory found their peace disturbed by fanatic fly and mosquito killers, intent on carrying out the instructions of their Chairman. The last sanctuary of individual freedom had been taken away.

The people's communes

Central to the whole concept of the Great Leap Forward was the grouping together of collectives into much larger units. The first one was created in Henan in April of 1958. It comprised 27 collectives with 9,369 households joined together, and was called Sputnik. Mao announced on 9th August that people's 'communes are good'. In the same month the Central Committee gave them official blessing:

> In the present circumstances, the establishment of people's communes with all-round management of agriculture, forestry, animal husbandry, side occupations, and fishery, where industry (the worker), agriculture (the peasant), exchange (the trader), culture and education (the student), and military affairs (the militiaman) merge into one, is the fundamental policy to guide the peasants to accelerate socialist construction, complete the building of socialism ahead of time, and carry out the gradual transition to Communism.

By December, 740,000 cooperatives had turned into 26,000 communes. The communes usually numbered around 20,000 and were coterminous with the smallest unit of the local government (the xiang) whose functions they replaced. Peasants' private plots were abolished as were private pigs and poultry. Even private eating and cooking were done away with. Large refectories provided food and there was no allocation of reward other than need. It was known as eating out of one big pot. Children were looked after in kindergartens releasing women for more labour. Women would no longer primarily serve their families but the state. Given the centrality of family life in China, it was a massive assault on traditional values. To Mao, it was the embodiment of Marxist morality: 'To each according to his need, from each according to his means.' It might even be possible to abolish money and thus to advance to a true Communist Society.

The communes were not only to produce food but also industrial goods and generate surpluses for use by the state. The theory was that all of this was spontaneous and a result of the will of the people whose energies would be unlocked by their direct involvement in these local units. In reality, the communes were controlled by the local cadres whose only interest was to extract as much labour and food from the reluctant peasants as possible. Family units resented the loss of ownership and richer villages resented sharing their produce with poorer neighbours, but fear and repression produced acquiescence. What was meant to be an experiment in democratic decentralisation was a return to the brutal mobilisation of labour by the state as practised by the first Qin Emperor or by the Sui who built the Grand Canal with forced labour. Mao was aware of the parallels and talked on one occasion of the need to avoid the fate of both these dynasties which were short lived.

The communes were also declared to be militia units and they were used as an instrument to militarise Chinese society. Communes were often referred to as military units subdivided into brigades and production teams were platoons. All between 15 and 50 years of age were to be militia members, and collections of weapons were to be kept by the communes and used in frequent training. There was to be a fighting style in the approach to work, platoons setting out together and returning together. Rising, eating and sleeping together would nurture military discipline. China had become one vast barracks.

THE GREAT LEAP FORWARD IN PRACTICE

The Central Committee meeting held in Wuhan in December 1958, when the triumphal completion of the commune forming process was announced was also the occasion of other news of importance. Mao Zedong was stepping down as Chairman of the People's Republic of China. It had been on the cards for some time. Mao disliked the formal duties of head of state. He was happiest in his dressing gown and slippers or swimming in one of the many pools provided for him. Day-to-day affairs could be left to the others, but he would still set the agenda. He became chairman of the Central Committee and therefore of the party. This is where power lay. He also remained chairman of the military affairs commission. Liu Shaoqi took over his role as head of state.

Agriculture and the Great Leap

This change did not mark an abandoning of the Great Leap. There were high hopes that the harvest would be a miraculous improvement on the usual. Close planting and deep ploughing had been urged on the farming communities as the secret of massive success. The normal yield was a ton per acre and the harvest of 1957 had seen a disappointing 195 million tons of grain across the country. There was talk of raising production from nine to 15 tons per acre in ordinary fields and even more staggering productivity increases in good areas. Mao announced at Wuhan that the harvest figure for 1958 was 430 million tons across the country. The party bureaucrats thought to play safe and publicly announced 375 million tons. In reality, this was far too high and eventually it was lowered to 250 million tons. Western experts place it at around 200 million tons. It ought to have been a record as the weather was superb. How had things gone wrong?

Part of the problem was the loss of statisticians in the anti-rightist campaign of 1957. Those left did not want to join ex-colleagues who had raised doubts in work detachments in inhospitable places. It was not good to be labelled a defeatist. At every level, officials lied and exaggerated. No commune wished to admit that it had not met its quota. Commune bosses forced production teams to exaggerate their output. **Jung Chang** in *Wild Swans: Three Daughters of China* (1991) gives one example of what must have been replicated across the country:

KEY PERSON

Jung Chang (1952–)
was the daughter of two communist intellectuals and therefore part of the ruling elite of the new China. She came to Britain after her family had suffered terribly in the Cultural Revolution and wrote her memoir, *Wild Swans: Three Daughters of China*, which was published in 1991. The book was an international best seller and as long as it is remembered that it is one person's view of events, it is a memorable and well-written insight into Mao's China.

In many places, people who refused to boast of massive increases in output were beaten up until they gave in. In Yibin, some leaders of production units were trussed up with their arms behind their backs in the village square while questions were hurled at them:

'How much wheat can you produce per mu?'

'Four hundred jin' (about 450 pounds – a realistic amount).

Then, beating him: 'How much wheat can you produce per mu?'

'Eight hundred jin.'

Even this impossible figure was not enough. The unfortunate man would be beaten, or simply left hanging, until he finally said: 'Ten thousand jin.' Sometimes the man died hanging there because he refused to increase the figure, or simply before he could raise the figure high enough.

Mao's doctor reported on the extraordinary lengths officials went to to keep up the pretence of success:

In Hubei, party secretary Ang Renzhong had ordered the peasants to remove rice plants from far-away fields and transplant them along Mao's route, to give the impression of a wildly abundant crop. The rice was planted so closely together that electric fans had to be set up around the fields to circulate air in order to prevent the plants from rotting. All of China was a stage, all the people performers in an extravaganza for Mao.

Those closest to Mao fed him a diet of flattery and tales of unadulterated success. His political secretary and the editor of *Red Flag*, the party's theoretical journal, Chen Boda, suggested that China was accomplishing in a day what it took capitalism 20 years to achieve.

If exaggeration was making much of a moderately good harvest in 1958, the harvest of 1959 was a disaster. The grain harvest fell to 170 million tons and in 1960 to 143 million tons. At the time, the harvest for 1959 was reported as 282 million tons and quotas were kept up on the communes. Grain exports to the USSR were actually increased to pay for heavy machinery. Close planting was producing soil exhaustion and the labour force was becoming increasingly exhausted as well. Endless military training, working on industrial development as well as increased agricultural work was taking its toll. Drought struck the north and floods the south. In 1960, it was worse. A hundred million acres were gripped by drought. It was possible to wade across the Yellow River in its lower reaches and in Shandong many rivers simply dried up. Floods later in the year devastated 50 million acres further south. The Mandate of Heaven seemed to have been withdrawn.

Industrialisation and the Great Leap

If the Great Leap Forward had not worked for agriculture, it was not very impressive in its industrial achievements either. There were some gains as local initiatives were encouraged in prospecting for and mining minerals. But the attempt to encourage diffused iron and steel production was a disaster. The encouragement to communes to produce their handicrafts and machinery needed steel, which was in short supply. Mao saw steel as the ultimate symbol of industrial development. The answer seemed to be local production: several hundred thousand blast furnaces and iron smelters were established across the country. Somewhere between 60 and 90 million people were drawn into the production process. By October 1958, 49 per cent of steel production was coming from small local furnaces. Mao's doctor recalls the absurdity of the process:

> *The backyard steel furnaces were equally disastrous. As the drive to produce steel continued at an ever more frenetic pace, people were forced to contribute their pots and pans, their doorknobs, the steel from their wrought-iron gates, shovels, and spades. There was not enough coal to fire the furnaces, so the fires were fed with the peasants' wooden furniture – their tables, chairs, and beds. But what came out of the furnaces was useless – nothing more than melted-down knives and pots and pans. Mao said that China was not on the verge of Communism, but in fact some absurd form of communism was already in place. Private property was being abolished, because private property was all being given away to feed the voracious steel furnaces.*

Even Mao had to admit at the Wuhan meeting in December that some of the steel was not of acceptable quality. Steel targets in 1959 were cut back. The diversion of labour into producing useless steel harmed the harvest which, in some cases, could not be gathered in. It also deprived many households of their woks and agricultural implements. The final blow to the dream of a massive increase in industrial production was the break with the USSR in 1960 (see Chapter 11). Aid ended and thousands of Soviet experts were withdrawn in June. The Great Leap Forward had ended in a shambles. The one senior leader who had tried to bring a dose of reality to proceedings early on was Peng Dehuai.

Peng Dehuai and the Lushun Conference

Mao and many others were beginning to have doubts about the reality of success by the spring of 1959. Food shortages had developed in the cities and it was obvious that estimates of production for both agricultural produce and industrial goods would have to be revised downwards. Mao, as always, displayed his knowledge of history and in an April meeting of the Central Committee referred to the well-known story of the Confucian official Hai Rui who had criticised a Ming Dynasty Emperor in the sixteenth century and been dismissed. He had announced that China needed more Hai Rui. When he got one, Mao changed his mind or at least simply behaved like his Ming predecessor. As so often in oppressive regimes, direct political points cannot be made. This tends to heighten the importance of the elliptical and indirect criticism through historical or literary analogies. Peng himself is supposed to have said at Lushun: 'I will play Hai Rui.' This did him no good and Mao clearly regretted his invoking of the event. In 1966, it was Mao's attack on a play, *The Dismissal of Hai Rui*, that launched the Cultural Revolution.

Peng Dehuai had a long history of clashing with Mao, but he was one of the undoubted heroes of communist China. Early in 1959, Peng had chosen to visit his birthplace in Hunan and talk to the peasants about the realities of the Great Leap Forward. He was appalled. Hunger, failure and waste, not heroic advance, marked his village. Peng reluctantly agreed to attend the leadership conference in Lushun in July and there was certainly no planned assault on Mao's authority on his part.

A chapter of accidents destroyed Peng. He tried to see Mao privately on Monday 13th July, but Mao was asleep. He then decided to commit his concerns to a private 'letter of opinion' to Mao. He sent it and Mao was outraged despite the fact that criticism of the Great Leap was mixed with praise for some aspects. Mao interpreted the criticism as an attack on his overall authority. He decided to circulate the letter to delegates, implying debate was acceptable, on 16th July, but then a few days later Mao launched an assault on Peng accusing him of being a 'right opportunist' and

Peng Duhuai at a soldier's meeting of People's Liberation Army (PLA) in 1948

forming an anti-party group. He challenged all the delegates to line up either with Mao or Peng. Peng was finished. He had been irretrievably damaged by a speech by Khrushchev on 18th July when the Russian leader had come out with many of the points Peng had made in criticism of China's approach to development. It looked as if Peng had briefed Khrushchev while on his travels in Europe that June. To criticise Mao and the party in private was one thing but to do so abroad another. On 30th July, a special meeting of the senior members of the Politburo was called and all except old Marshal Zhu De lined up with Mao. Peng was sacked as Minister of Defence and replaced by Lin Biao. He was finished as a major political figure, but his past record saved him for the time being from a worse fate. His fall ushered in a wave of persecutions of so-called 'right opportunists', who were not as lucky as Peng. Special camps and hard labour awaited them. It was dangerous to criticise the emperor. The affair had the unfortunate effect of polarising opinion and making criticism of the Great Leap Forward dangerous. It gave the fanatics a new lease of life and kept the policies going just when there was a growing sense in the leadership that they needed modifying. Mao dug his heels in, refusing initially to accept failure and, in 1960, was talking of extending communes to the cities.

'Hungry Ghosts – China's Secret Famine'

KEY TERM

Hungry Ghosts – China's Secret Famine is a recent account of this greatest of twentieth-century tragedies by Jasper Becker. It was published in 1996.

The ultimate condemnation of the Great Leap Forward lies in the horrific famine that resulted. A recent account of the famine bears the title *Hungry Ghosts*. It was not wholly man-made or Mao-made; dreadful weather in 1959 and again in 1960 partly accounts for it. Nevertheless, as many Chinese authorities have since admitted, it was 70 per cent due to human incompetence. It was the worst famine of the twentieth century and somewhere between 20 and 30 million people starved to death, yet there was no word of it in the west at the time and no appeal came from the Chinese government for help. It was not until 1980 that the famine was officially recognised in China as having taken place.

Even in December 1958 there were food shortages developing in the cities and throughout 1959 these grew worse. The food allowances in towns steadily declined to a level comparable or lower than those given to the inmates of Auschwitz. In parts of the countryside, it was worse as grain procurements continued. In 1960, it was catastrophic with mass starvation widespread; in 1961, five million people died of hunger. Children were particularly affected. Where the real leftist believers among the party had promoted the Great Leap with the greatest fanaticism in Sichuan and Anhui provinces, 10–20 per cent of the population died of hunger. People ate bark and grass and in some areas their own children. Bandits multiplied, often ex-militiamen of the cursed communes. Women and children were sold by husbands and fathers. Punishments for theft of food in the communes was savage. Two children trying to steal food had wires pushed through their ears and were then hung by the wires from a wall. Fingers were lopped off and noses cut. It was a return to the most savage times of a brutal past. Mao was increasingly depressed. He took to his bed for long periods and according to his doctor gave up eating meat as a gesture of sympathy.

CONCLUSION

The Great Leap Forward stands as a monument to the stupidities of misplaced idealism. It is an awful warning of what happens when fanatics without the restraints of a free press and representative institutions experiment on mankind. Lenin, Hitler and Stalin had all tried to fulfil their dreams of utopia with horrific consequences for their people. Mao and his colleagues, with more people to play with, killed even more. The leadership cut itself off from reality and believed what it wanted to believe. At every level down the chain of command, officials joined in the pretence of success. No one dared to speak the truth. It was too dangerous. Mao's faith in mass mobilisation and contempt for experts produced millions of tons of useless iron. Ordinary people had their lives wrecked by the arrogance of men who thought they had the answer.

Two outcomes of the Great Leap might be considered achievements. In Beijing, the ancient walls were pulled down and the vast Tiananmen Square laid out as a monument to the grandeur of the new China. The other was the starting of China's nuclear programme and in 1964, this led to the successful explosion of a Chinese atom bomb. Both indicate the priorities of the regime.

SUMMARY QUESTIONS

1 Why was the Great Leap Forward launched in 1958?

2 Describe the role of communes in the Great Leap Forward?

3 What accounts for the failure of the Great Leap Forward?

4 Why did Mao Zedong react with such hostility to the criticisms of Peng Dehuai?

TIMELINE

1957	Anti-rightist campaign intimidates intellectuals
April 1958	First commune
May 1958	Official launch of Great Leap Forward
December 1958	Wuhan Conference; communes cover China
1959	Famine begins
July 1959	Lushun Conference; Peng Dehuai tries to reason with Mao
1960	Natural disasters; famine worsens
June 1960	Russians withdraw experts; Great Leap Forward ends

CHAPTER 10

Recovery and revolution: China, 1961–69

INTRODUCTION

These eight years are marked by dramatic changes of direction in policy and an increasingly bitter power struggle. Great issues of principle were completely intertwined with a crude clash of personalities. The disasters stemming from the Great Leap Forward led many in the party to question Mao's judgement. Mao was inclined to gloss over the disaster and see it as an unfortunate hiccup in the achievement of his egalitarian utopia. He still remained committed to the pursuit of equality even when equality seemed to mean equal misery for all. Initially, he was forced to retreat and compromise but in 1966 launched one of the most extraordinary examples of mass mobilisation in the history of humanity, the Great Cultural Revolution. It swept away his political rivals and while reducing China to anarchy in many areas, transformed Mao into a god.

RECOVERY, 1961–65

There was much to recover from. Wholesale social breakdown threatened in 1960–61. Bandits once more terrorised vast areas. Armed revolt broke out in many of the worst affected provinces like Sichuan and far-away Tibet. In Shandong, there was simply chaotic anarchy. It was as it had been in the declining days of the Qing Dynasty. Many must have wondered if the Mandate of Heaven had been withdrawn from the Communist regime. The new dynasty had behaved like the brutal but short-lived Sui and Qin Dynasties and Mao himself had been aware of the ominous parallels. What was needed was wise counsel from the emperor's mandarins, but would the Emperor listen?

The wise mandarins were to hand. Liu Shaoqi was aware of the mistakes made as was the subtle and pliant Zhou Enlai. Deng Xiaoping, the party general secretary, had also lost some of his faith in the wise proceedings of

Mao. He had been an enthusiastic supporter of mass mobilisation in 1958. In 1962, he recanted and in a speech to the Communist Youth League announced a very un-Maoist approach. Fanaticism was out and **pragmatism** was in.

> 'Whether white or black, a cat is a good cat so long as it catches the rat.' The reason why we were able to defeat Chiang Kaishek was that we did not use conventional methods ... and always took account of circumstances ... In present conditions, both in industry and agriculture, we cannot advance without taking a step back. Do you not see this? Isn't agriculture going backwards? Are the communes not in retreat? The first step now must be to restore grain crops and to replenish the stocks of agricultural implements and draught animals ... In the past, we had too many movements. We had movements all the time and all those movements were national movements. This clearly didn't work.

All through 1961 and early 1962 there was a steady retreat from the idiocies of the Great Leap Forward. In April 1961, it was accepted that communal mess halls were not working well and were unpopular. Suddenly, priority was given to manufacturing pots and woks given up to make useless iron. Peasants would need them to cater for themselves once more, assuming that is that there was any food. Small private plots were restored and the amount of land for such use increased. Fairs and markets and peddlers were allowed again and something like a free market economy began to emerge on a small scale. Already many communes had fragmented into smaller units. In September 1961, the basic unit of production once again became the production team of around 30 households. This was a reversion to the system based on single collectivised villages. Rewards were to be based on effort and work. No longer was it the Marxist credo of 'to each according to his needs, from each according to his means'. No work meant no food. The 'big pot' was no more.

In some areas, this was not enough, and Zhu De, after a visit to his native Sichuan, reported that many peasants were simply reverting to private farming and it seemed to be working. He argued that since the peasants were

Pragmatism means acting not according to abstract principles but according to the needs and circumstances of the time. Deng Xiaoping's 'black cat/white cat' speech became famous as the expression of a pragmatic approach which finally triumphed in the 1980s with enormous beneficial effects.

doing it anyway, the party might as well go along with it. Mao was horrified and saw not only the communes collapsing but even the smaller scale collectivisation of the early 1950s. Gradually, production increased and by 1965, the grain harvest was back to what it had been in 1957. In the meantime, to alleviate the shortages, six million tons of grain was imported from the capitalist west, mainly from Canada and Australia but indirectly even from the hated USA.

In industry as well there was a greater realism. There was a shift in emphasis to light industry and year by year planning replaced five-year planning to give greater flexibility. Deng, Chen Yun and Bo Yibo produced new guidelines for industry, abandoning Mao's schemes of 1960. Back came hierarchy, respect for experts and wage differentials to provide incentives. Loss-making plants were closed and realistic targets set. It worked, and by 1965, levels of industrial output were nearly double that of 1957. The price of all of this was a retreat from socialist idealism and Mao was not happy.

Recovery was also marked by a political liberalisation. There was a more positive view taken of intellectuals. At a conference on science and technology in 1962, vice premier Chen Yi said:

> *There is something other people won't dare to say, but I will ... China needs intellectuals, needs scientists. For all these years, they have been unfairly treated. They should be restored to the position they deserve.*

Premier Zhou at the same meeting echoed the same message of friendship. Many of the purged right opportunists of 1959 were quietly rehabilitated from April onwards under the direction of Liu Shaoqi – he did not ask for Mao's approval. There was, in fact, as Jung Chang records in her book, *Wild Swans: Three Daughters of China* (1991), a general thaw that in some ways looked forward to the 1980s, a decade without Mao:

> *For my father and mother, as for many others, the regime seemed to be showing it could correct and learn from its mistakes and that it could work – and this restored their confidence in it.*

THE POWER STRUGGLE, 1962–65

However, Mao was there in 1962 and could not be overlooked. He was the embodiment of the revolution and could not be removed without threatening the legitimacy of the whole regime. He was also a consummate political operative as he had shown time and time again. The issues at stake were about fundamental policies and personal power. Mao had to accept in 1961 that some retreat was necessary from the policies that had brought about the crisis, but he did not accept that they were fundamentally flawed. He retained his faith in mass mobilisation, equality in all things and a deep distrust of hierarchy and experts. To Mao, as he got older, the correct ideological approach seemed to matter more than results. Once he had denounced 'dogma as dog shit', now he was increasingly appalled by the approach of Deng and Liu. The colour of the cat seemed to matter more to Mao than whether it could catch mice. At times, he was inclined to argue that the loss of life was inevitable in the achievement of a great goal. One of Mao's close associates, Chen Boda, dismissed the famine as 'an unavoidable phenomenon in our forward march'. Chen Boda organised a special meeting in 1962 of 'true left' intellectuals and Mao addressed them with a very different emphasis from that of premier Zhou and vice premier Chen Yi from intellectuals earlier in the year:

> *Intellectuals work in offices ... They live well, eat well, dress well. They don't walk very much. This is why they often catch colds ... Things are getting complicated now ... Some people are talking about a household contract system, which is really nothing but a revival of capitalism. We have governed this country for all these years, but we are still able to control only two thirds of our society. One third remains in the hands of our enemy or sympathizers of our enemy. The enemy can buy people off, not to mention all those comrades who have married the daughters of landlords.*

The opening round in the power struggle went badly wrong for Mao. He called a Central Committee meeting which would also be attended by leading party officials from the provinces. It was known as the 7,000 Cadres meeting and was held in January and early

Liu Shaoqi and **Deng Xiaoping** headed the party bureaucracy. Liu had replaced Mao as Chairman of the republic and Deng was general secretary of the party. They accepted the Socialist Education Movement but with a different purpose and emphasis from Mao.

A whole series of documents Initially representing the Mao line, the guidelines were the Early Ten Points. This was replaced by the secretariat in September 1963 with the Later Ten Points. This gave way to the Revised Later Ten Points in 1964, still essentially the Deng and Liu line. Mao had these withdrawn and, in 1965, replaced it with a document called the Twenty-three Articles, which was essentially a return to the original. It was now that reference was made to the struggle between the two roads.

The downfall of Khrushchev Khrushchev had emerged after 1953 as Stalin's successor as general secretary and from 1957 seemed the unchallenged boss of the Soviet Union. He became associated with a series of agricultural blunders such as 'maize mania' and the Virgin Lands scheme and rather clownish international behaviour. By October 1964, his sedate colleagues in the renamed Politburo had had enough, and in a sudden move when he was on holiday, dethroned him.

February 1962. Mao intended it to draw a line under past failure and also put a stop to the drift away from socialism. In the event, it turned into a very disagreeable experience. He was appalled by the speech given by his deputy, Liu Shaoqi, accepting that the party was to blame for widespread failure. Whether Liu actually deceived Mao by delivering a different speech from the one Mao had seen, as Jung Chang suggests, or he had simply not read the speech, as Doctor Li suggests, all agree he was dismayed and found the mood of criticism deeply troubling. He made a half-hearted self-criticism later in the proceedings and then retired to his room grumbling about the delegates. Far from stopping the drift from socialism, it speeded it up and by the summer of 1962, 20 per cent of Chinese agriculture had reverted to the 'personal responsibility system'. Mao decided to take a long holiday and sulked.

He did not give up, however. Under his prodding, the **Socialist Education Movement** was launched in May 1963. The movement was accepted by the party mandarins, but their approach was very different. The movement's aim was to reinvigorate the local parties with the socialist and collectivist ethic. Mao wanted rectification from below with struggle meetings against party officials as there had been struggle meetings against landlords in the early 1950s. Deng Xiaoping and Liu wanted rectification from above, with work teams sent out from the centre to assess corruption and abuse of power rather than ideological purity. A **whole series of documents** was issued in the name of the Central Committee reflecting first the Mao approach then that of Deng and Liu. Mao began to talk of the two lines or two roads, the capitalist road and the socialist road. He was increasingly convinced that Deng and Liu were not dependable.

There was also a simple struggle for power. Mao resented his loss of authority. 'They treat me like a dead ancestor,' he famously complained. There was respect, but he was not consulted as much as he would have liked. **The downfall of Khrushchev** in October 1964 particularly worried him. He disliked the Soviet leader and did not regret his going but that the Soviet Politburo, now renamed the Presidium, could topple the leader so easily was shocking. Who would be the Chinese Brezhnev? Mao's concerns must have been heightened by the remarks of the Russian Defence Minister to a visiting Chinese delegation in November 1964. 'We've got rid of our fool Khrushchev, now you get rid of yours, Mao,' Marshal Malinovsky is reported as saying to Marshal Ho Lung of the People's Liberation Army (PLA). The charges against Khrushchev of bungling and messing up agriculture must have looked particularly ominous to Mao.

Tensions with his own nominated successor clearly increased in 1965. In January, Liu Shaoqi called a National Assembly meeting. It was largely a ceremonial body that elected the President. He had himself re-elected in a blaze of glory, very different from when he had taken over in 1959. There was even some talk of hanging just his portrait on the Tiananmen Gate without Mao's. Liu sensibly vetoed the idea. Chairman Mao was jealous enough as it was. He talked of Deng and Liu running independent kingdoms.

The importance of Lin Biao and the PLA

Mao, however, was hardly powerless. His prestige was still enormous and he skilfully built up rival power centres to those of Deng and Liu. The most important of these was the PLA under Lin Biao, who became increasingly important at this time. Lin Biao is a somewhat controversial figure. Was he a Machiavellian schemer plotting his way to the throne like a Chinese Richard III, or as **Frederick Teiwes** and **Warren Sun** have indicated in their book *The Tragedy of Lin Biao*, a rather sad and exploited figure used by Mao and his own wife in the cause of their ambitions? Lin, as indicated earlier, had been a brilliant soldier and was undoubtedly one of the heroes of the revolution. He had been badly wounded in 1938, and after the civil war, appears to have been frequently ill. He did not play a major role in politics in the 1950s but was brought back to prominence by Mao at the Lushun Conference in 1959. He delivered a fulsome speech in praise of Mao and thus helped to destroy his fellow marshal, Peng Dehuai, whose position he inherited as Minister of Defence.

KEY PEOPLE

Frederick C Teiwes and **Warren Sun's** work, *The Tragedy of Lin Biao: Riding the Tiger during the Cultural Revolution* (1996), challenges the official Chinese line on Lin and that popular in the west, that Lin was an ambitious political schemer.

Thereafter, the one principle of his political life was to agree with Mao. At the 7,000 Cadres Conference of January 1962, Lin delivered gushing praise of Mao, and more than any of the other leaders, seemed to have denied that the Great Leap was such an abysmal failure. The speech was not popular, but Mao clapped enthusiastically. As head of the PLA, Lin stressed the primacy of ideology and correct thought, and to produce this, he suggested a short compilation of Mao's sayings, which became the famous **Little Red Book**. This was issued to all recruits, and the PLA rapidly became Mao's favourite institution. No compliment for the Chairman was too extreme for Lin Biao: 'Mao Zedong's thought is the highest peak in the world today.' His education programme in the PLA attracted special praise from the emperor. Learn from the PLA was his response. Lin, in fact, was taking Mao's cult of personality to new heights. China's model citizen came to be a fictitious PLA soldier, Lei Feng, whose invented diary was used as a source of propaganda:

> *I felt particularly happy this morning when I got up, because last night I had dreamed of our great leader, Chairman Mao. And it so happens that today is the Party's 40th anniversary. Today I have so much to tell the party, so much gratitude to the Party … I am like a toddler, and the Party is like my mother who helps me, and teaches me to walk … My beloved Party, my loving mother, I am always your loyal son.*

In 1965, Lin moved the PLA closer still to the Maoist theoretical model of equality with simplification of officers' uniforms and a renewed political education drive. Correct thought was placed first as the most desirable quality in a soldier. This was a far cry from Deng's indifference to a cat's colour as long as it caught mice. Basically, with Lin Biao in charge of the PLA, Mao was creating a strong counterweight to those he considered revisionists in the party hierarchy.

Other allies and Jiang Qing

Three other individuals were to achieve prominence and power as allies of Mao. Chen Boda, his political secretary, was increasingly used, as was the sinister Kang Sheng, trained by the NKVD, the Soviet secret police, in police work and who had been in charge of the physical side of

---

KEY EVENT

The **Little Red Book** was produced in its millions. It was an essential item for all Red Guards. Reading extracts of Mao's thoughts was seen as wonder-working. Ludicrous stories circulated of improved performance in all manner of fields after reading some saying of Mao. Lin Biao's wife regularly reminded her husband of the need to have it with him when leaving for work.

the rectification campaign in Yan'an during the war. These two were to be particularly useful to Mao in passing on his wishes. Another even closer figure who assumed political importance for the first time in the 1960s was Mao's wife.

Jiang Qing, the infamous Madame Mao, was the Chairman's most loyal supporter for the simple reason that Mao was the only reason she had any importance. They had been married since 1939, but any personal closeness had ended long ago. Mao satisfied himself with a series of young women while pleading impotence to his wife. Madame Mao had other uses and during 1962–63 she gradually became more prominent in the arts and culture. She had been an actress in Shanghai before the war with a dubious political and sexual past, but by the 1960s she was China's most devoted Maoist promoting revolutionary orthodoxy on the stage and on the written page. The result was a dull theatre of stylised heroics. Her views are revealed in an argument that developed with Mao's doctor after seeing a classic Chinese opera in which a ghost appeared. Ghosts were somehow bourgeois and anti-Communist and as such should cease to exist on stage, screen or on paper. Dr Li records her saying: *'Talking about ghosts promotes superstition. It's not good for the common people.'*

Dr Li reminded her that Shakespeare's Hamlet has a ghost. This made no impact on her and she retorted:

> *Just because Shakespeare's plays have ghosts doesn't mean we have to have ghosts. The chairman has discovered many problems in literature and art that indicate serious class conflict. You had better pay attention to my words.*

It was an argument over a play that was to light the fuse that exploded the Cultural Revolution underneath the bourgeois Deng Xiaoping and Liu Shaoqi and the other capitalist roadsters (the term used at the time) at party headquarters.

SETTING OFF THE CULTURAL REVOLUTION, FEBRUARY 1965 – AUGUST 1966

With great cunning Mao moved slowly and indirectly to confront his opponents. He always believed that in warfare a good general should circle around. Madame Mao was dispatched in February 1965 to Shanghai to commission an article attacking the historian, bureaucrat and playwright Wu Han. Wu Han had turned his book on the dismissal of Hai Rui into a play. Mao had initially found no fault, but the parallels with Peng Dehuai were too great and he became convinced that it was an attack on him. Wu Han was a close colleague of Peng Zhen, the mayor of Beijing who was himself a close ally of Liu Shaoqi.

The attack was published in a Shanghai newspaper in November. Peng forbad any Beijing paper to reprint the article. Again, Mao showed cunning. Instead of overruling Peng, he got Zhou Enlai to do the job for him and argue that it was simply a literary issue, and therefore, that it should be debated. In February 1966, the whole issue was broadened out by a document issued jointly by Jiang Qing and the PLA. It criticised much culture promoted by the party since 1949 as anti-socialist and contrary to Mao's thought. The next move was carefully timed with Liu Shaoqi's absence abroad. It was a frontal assault on Peng Zhen carried out by Mao's two attack dogs, Kang Sheng and Chen Boda. Mao distanced himself and withdrew to Shanghai. The two persuaded the Politburo that Peng had mishandled the matter and should resign. Liu returned to find that his first task was to dismiss his loyal colleague and supporter. Deng Xiaoping and Zhou Enlai had decided to sacrifice Peng, and Liu went along with it. None of them appreciated what Mao was up to. He had achieved a major victory in removing the political boss of Beijing and he now pushed his advantage.

On 16th May, an enlarged Politburo meeting approved a circular which launched the Cultural Revolution:

> *Representatives of the bourgeoisie have sneaked into our party. They are a bunch of counter-revolutionary revisionists. Some of these people have already been exposed. Others have not.*

Deng and Liu clearly hoped to bring any rectification movement under their control by operating any changes through centrally appointed work teams. Mao and his supporters had other ideas. They would appeal over the heads of the party establishment to the people and in particular to young people. Lin Biao's speech on 18th May began this appeal. He started with his usual adulation of Chairman Mao which sank to a new low of ghastly grovelling. The phrase **Red Guards** was coined at the end of the month and Kang Sheng, through his wife, orchestrated a poster campaign at Beijing University to rouse up the students. Deng and Liu tried to fight back and made Red Guard organisations illegal. Unfortunately for them, Mao and his allies controlled the PLA and the internal security apparatus.

To complete the discomfiture of perceived enemies in the party apparatus, Mao now grandly decided to return like an exiled god to retake command of heaven. He announced his renewed power and vigour with a swim in the Yangtze at Wuhan. It was no mean feat for a 72-year-old to swim several miles in the fast-flowing Yangtze. Lack of courage had never been one of Mao's failings.

On his arrival in Beijing, he called a special Central Committee meeting, the first since his humiliation in 1962. This was to be a very different affair. Additional members were added with instructions to cheer Lin and Mao and jeer any opponents. The meeting launched the Cultural Revolution with an assault on the Four Olds – old culture, old ideas, old customs and old habits. The distribution of power was radically altered. Lin Biao became number two on the standing committee and Liu fell from number two to number eight. On 18th August, Mao presided over the first of eight giant rallies of Red Guards in Tiananmen Square.

There was one last centre of resistance. Provincial party secretaries and their organisations resisted the Red Guards and in October, Mao called them to a conference in Beijing. After initial resistance, Mao and his allies broke Liu and Deng by insisting that they make abject self-criticism in front of the assembly. They did in extravagant form. Both then disappeared from public view in December, **Deng** for six years, **Liu** forever. Mao had won the power struggle.

KEY TERM

Red Guards (hongweibing in Chinese) was coined towards the end of May at Qinghua University, the starting and finishing point of the Cultural Revolution. Students and schoolchildren formed themselves into Red Guard units to terrorise opponents of Chairman Mao's thought. Ritual humiliation, the use of the jet plane position and sometimes fatal torture were all employed. Sometimes, the Red Guards chose their own victims; at other times, they were directed by agents of Jiang Qing and Kang Sheng.

CHAOS AND CONFUSION: THE CULTURAL REVOLUTION, AUGUST 1966 – APRIL 1969

KEY EVENTS

Liu Shaoqi was obviously Mao's most eminent victim. He was under house arrest from early 1967, but from April the treatment got steadily worse. He died of pneumonia and deliberate neglect in 1969, lying in excrement in a cold cell. His wife was in prison for eight years.

Deng Xiaoping was also attacked after a period under house arrest. He was made to kneel in the jet plane position in July 1967 but avoided further physical abuse. His son was not so lucky and was thrown from a high window. Deng was eventually sent to Jiangxi under house arrest and performed part-time manual labour at a nearby factory.

Red Guards units multiplied throughout August 1966. By the end of the year, all schools and colleges were closed for revolutionary struggle. Free travel was announced on the railways for Red Guards. Teachers, in particular, bore much of the brunt of the initial violence. Since 1980, a series of memoirs have appeared, all tending to emphasise the true horror and mindless violence of events in these years. Perhaps the most famous in Britain is Jung Chang's *Wild Swans: Three Daughters of China* (1991) referred to earlier. She describes the assault on her philosophy teacher:

> *In the centre my teacher was being kicked around, rolling in agony on the floor, her hair askew. As she cried out, begging them to stop, the boys who had set upon her said in cold voices, 'Now you beg! Haven't you been ferocious? Now beg properly!' They kicked her again, and ordered her to kowtow to them and say 'Please spare my life, masters!' To make someone kowtow and beg was an extreme humiliation. She sat up and stared blankly ahead: I met her eyes through her knotted hair. In them I saw agony, desperation, and emptiness.*

Elsewhere, teachers were tortured to death by enraged pupils for no better reason than the memory of some past hurt or humiliation. One primary school headmaster was killed and then eaten by his pupils in one of the more remote provinces. Intellectuals of all sorts were liable to attract attention. China's leading novelist, Lao She, author of *Rickshaw* and a voluntary returnee to China in 1949, was so badly beaten (and forced to burn his books and manuscripts) that he committed suicide.

Houses were broken into and pillaged of suspicious materials, often books and works of art. Anything that could be labelled foreign or capitalist was suspect. Books were confiscated and burnt. One householder was victimised for having a sofa and matching chairs, a particularly bourgeois crime. One pianist had his fingers broken for playing Chopin.

Workers' groups began to copy the children and students and form their own units of Red Guards. The sheer lunacy and uncontrolled aggression was reminiscent of other collective outbreaks of madness in the past. It shared many of the characteristics of the Boxer Rising and the Taiping Rebellion in the nineteenth century. Even the language used was often similar. There was much talk of destroying snake heads and demons. The police did not intervene and anarchy quickly developed nationwide. The cities, particularly Beijing and Shanghai, were the most affected.

Gangs of Red Guards were soon fighting pitched battles and inflicting the most ghastly atrocities on one another. Children could suffer for any imagined short-coming on their own behalf or because of their parents. Gao Yuan recalls many such incidents:

> When I looked at Zongwei's bare legs ... they were riddled with holes the diameter of a pencil, surrounded by strings of loose flesh the consistency of shredded pork. Blood and puss oozed from the wounds. 'What in hell did they use on him,' Dr Yang muttered. Looking round the room, I found the answer to her question: the pokers used to tend the stove.

Inevitably, in such an atmosphere of chaos the most brutal and criminal often rose to the top and used the whole episode as camouflage for robbery. Mao seemed unconcerned. Some must die in any creative process was his approach.

Violence probably reached a climax in January 1967. Shanghai was paralysed by a strike, with diminishing food supplies and fighting between rival factions of Red Guards. Mao gave the first indication at this time that things were perhaps going too far and senior figures in the PLA took this as a sign to launch the February crackdown. In fact, it was Mao playing his old game of moving first one way, then another, to control events. The Cultural Revolution had still not done its work in rectifying the party and Mao signalled that the crackdown had been too severe and over-enthusiastic commanders in the PLA were punished for being too repressive.

By September 1967, even Mao seemed to have reached the conclusion that anarchy had gone too far and it was time to restore discipline and rebuild the party structure. The process was heavily reliant on Lin Biao and the PLA. The events of the summer seem to have united all the surviving figures of authority and convinced them that total breakdown might ensue. In the large industrial Yangtze city of Wuhan, full-scale fighting developed between two factions and also the army which sided with one of them. Hundreds were killed and in the province as a whole,184,000 people were injured. In August, a radical group seized the foreign ministry and attacked the British embassy. Mao after moving from one side to the other – between the radicals and the PLA – finally came down on the side of order and backed Zhou and Lin Biao to restore discipline. Throughout 1968, the PLA slowly restored order. Full-scale civil war in Shensi was smothered and the theft and use of heavy weaponry in the southern province of Guangxi restored to its proper intended purpose of transfer to the North Vietnamese. The final struggle was to bring the Red Guards of Qinhua University in Beijing under control. This was achieved in July. Over the next two years, five million young people were sent for compulsory re-education into the countryside.

The Ninth Party Congress in April 1969 might be said to mark the end of the most violent phase of the Cultural Revolution. The Congress was a total triumph for Mao. Mao's thought was once again enshrined as the guiding ideology of China. The cult of his personality reached new depths of absurdity. Liu Shaoqi was denounced as 'a hidden traitor and scab'. Lin Biao was named as Mao's anointed successor and close comrade in arms. The Congress marked the triumph of the PLA. Over half the delegates were wearing army uniforms. The old Central Committee had been destroyed with less than a quarter re-elected to the new one, which was dominated by the army who composed 45 per cent of the 279 members. The 25-man Politburo contained nine serving soldiers and three former marshals. The once-powerful secretariat had all but disappeared.

MAKING SENSE OF THE CULTURAL REVOLUTION

Why did these horrific series of events unfold is the basic question to be asked. The answer is simple – Mao. But two other important questions then need to be answered and the answers are much more complex. Why did Mao want to launch the Cultural Revolution in the way he did? Why was he able to do so?

Most historians would agree with Richard Evans, the former British ambassador to China and the author of an excellent biography of Deng Xiaoping: 'Mao planned it, launched it and had a greater hand in directing it than anyone else.' His motives appear to have been mixed. At one level, it was a simple power struggle between political rivals. Mao resented the shadow emperor Liu Shaoqi and wished him removed. He resented and feared any other potential rivals, particularly anyone who might be seen as working with the Russians to dethrone him. The words of Marshal Malinovsky to He Lung were not forgotten and were probably He Lung's death warrant. He was tortured and died of medical neglect. Peng Dehuai had four ribs broken under torture. He later died in a prison hospital. Li Lisan, leader of the party in 1928 was killed in 1967. All who had crossed Mao, as well as many who had not, disappeared, died or suffered maltreatment. In this sense, the Cultural Revolution was a resounding success for Mao. It left him as unchallenged emperor. The endless cries of '10,000 years to [Chairman Mao]' were the words traditionally used to greet the emperors of old.

It was, however, more than just a political struggle between personalities. In one sense, it was the logical outcome of the Socialist Education Movement, representing the triumph of Mao's approach of rectification from below rather than discipline from above, as Liu and Deng wanted. It embodied Mao's essential faith in popular involvement and mass mobilisation and his distrust of the intelligentsia. It promoted equality in many respects. To many rural areas the new **barefoot doctors** were as much the symbol of these years as the Red Guards. Here Mao claimed he was tackling the elitism of the medical profession with their long period of training and their tendency to ignore the

KEY TERM

Barefoot doctors were hastily trained nurses with simple medical techniques who were intended to raise health standards in rural areas where there were few real doctors.

peasants and focus on the cities. Even the dispatch of urban Red Guards, composed of the children of the intelligentsia, to work in villages was part of his drive for equality between town and country.

If the Cultural Revolution was partly naked power struggle and partly a battle of ideas, it also sprang from Mao's complex psyche and personal needs. Mao's behaviour was filled with ludicrous contradictions. He mocked books and old culture and applauded the Red Guards who wrecked libraries and burnt private collections. Yet, he himself lived surrounded by books and passed his time reading the classics of Chinese literature and writing poetry in classical forms. In his article 'Revolutionary Immortality: Mao Tse-Tung and the Cultural Revolution' (1968), the US psychiatrist Robert J Lifton saw Mao's embracing of youth, rebellion and excitement as the lament of an old man approaching the grave. He has also been seen by some commentators as **Mao the 'Monkey King'**. Sun the Monkey King, with his red behind, was the hero of one of Mao's favourite novels, *Journey to the West*. He performs incredible feats, showing respect to no one. Mao himself said of these years: 'We've been the Monkey King upsetting heaven.' Perhaps the whole Cultural Revolution was the ultimate existentialist experience –fun; full of sound and fury but essentially signifying nothing.

CONCLUSION

Whatever Mao's motives in launching the Cultural Revolution, it is necessary to consider what made it possible. Firstly, Mao's own prestige and power within the party. If he set his mind to it, it was difficult for the party to resist. The party's fate and its authority was bound up with those of Mao after years of his cult of personality. He could not lose the Mandate of Heaven without removing it from the party. Individual party members proved spineless in coordinating resistance. Chief among them was Zhou Enlai whose golden rule of survival was not to oppose Mao. The fiendishly clever and indirect way by which Mao proceeded, using his wife Jiang Qing, the security chief Kang Sheng and, most importantly, Lin Biao and the PLA, all made it hard to resist. He also tapped into all the resentments and petty personal differences within the party hierarchy. Old scores could be paid off and promotion achieved by jumping on to the Cultural Revolutionary band wagon. In calling up the popular enthusiasm of the young and later that of workers, Mao was tapping into bottled-up resentments of an over-controlled society with no outlets for feelings and rebellion. There were none of those outlets that the young in the west might have, for example in popular music and sport. Workers had no free trade unions to tackle their managers and peasants had no redress against party cadres who were seen as responsible for all the miseries of the Great Leap Forward. Suddenly, no less a person than the emperor had announced that 'it is right to rebel'; it was right to 'bombard party headquarters'. All the traditional authority of Mao, the older brother, the national father figure was placed behind expressing resentment. The cork was pulled out of the bottle by the man who had done most to put it in.

The results of the Cultural Revolution were almost wholly negative. The best estimates of numbers of deaths is half a million. Many times these had suffered torture and beatings. Millions of both party functionaries and later Red Guards had been sent into the country for re-education via hard labour. Industrial output had fallen by 14 per cent in 1967 and fell again in 1968. Agriculture was far less damaged, if at all. The education of millions had been adversely affected by the closure and disruption to schools and later the punishment of radical activists. Many of those sent to the countryside were not to return till the late 1970s. Culture and the arts, in the grip of Jiang Qing, were a dreary example of agitprop (political propaganda pretending to be art) at its worst. She had used her power not only to promote a mindless worship of Mao and the all consuming importance of class struggle but also to pay off old scores and persecute anyone who had ever slighted her.

Mao was more a demi-god than ever, but the other chief gainers were Lin Biao and the PLA. To destroy his rivals in the party, Mao had had to promote that other institution on which the new dynasty rested, the army. China was now a more militarised society than ever. Zhou Enlai had survived, still at the centre. He had done

HEINEMANN ADVANCED HISTORY

1959–61 Economic Crisis

1962   7,000 Cadres
        meeting; Mao
        makes self-criticism

1963   Socialist Education
        Movement started

1964   Fall of Khrushchev

1965   Jiang Qing and Lin
        Biao work together
        on culture and
        propaganda; affair of
        Han Rui begins

1966   Fall of Peng Zhen
        and launch of
        Cultural Revolution

1967   Climax of violence –
        Shanghai (January),
        Wuhan (July)

1968   PLA restores order

1969   Ninth Congress.
        Lin Biao named as
        Mao's heir

his best to minimise disruption and where possible to protect people like Deng Xiaoping. His survival was to prove crucial.

SUMMARY QUESTIONS

1 By what means did Liu Shaoqi, Deng Xiaoping and Zhou Enlai try to bring about economic recovery in the years 1961–65?

2 Why did Mao Zedong launch the Cultural Revolution in 1966?

3 Why were Liu Shaoqi and Deng Xiaoping defeated in 1965–66?

4 What were the consequences of the Cultural Revolution by 1969?

CHAPTER 11

China and the world, 1949–76

INTRODUCTION

China's relations with the rest of the world were determined by the complex interplay of many forces, ideas and traditions. Initially, many in the west interpreted the new China purely in terms of the ideological confrontation, known as the **Cold War.** The new Chinese government proclaimed itself Communist. It claimed Marxist–Leninism as its official ideology and claimed to support world revolution. The imperialist powers led by the USA were denounced. The USSR was proclaimed a friend. Mao spoke in 1949 of 'leaning to one side'. He argued:

> We belong to the anti-imperialist front headed by the USSR, and we can look for genuine friendly aid only from that front.

In the USA, the 'loss' of China to Communism fuelled the ardour of militant anti-Communists, like Senator Joseph Macarthy, who were determined to see the world in Manichean terms. On the one side, freedom, democracy and capitalism led and protected by Uncle Sam and, on the other, totalitarian, socialist slavery pushed like some damaging drug by the arch-crook in the Kremlin, Joseph Stalin. Mao and the new Chinese regime were seen by these increasingly influential cold warriors as Stalin's Asian side-kicks, no more, no less.

This analysis of China's stance was, of course, a gross simplification. Mao felt considerable distrust of Stalin. The Russian dictator had let him down frequently. Russian aid in the civil war, while useful, was far from decisive. Even in the spring of 1949, Stalin was urging the Communists to limit their power to the area north of the Yangtze. Mao talked of 'leaning' to the Soviet side, not accepting Soviet domination. There were several points of dispute between Russia and China. Russia was occupying parts of Xinjiang in the far west and had staked various economic claims on Manchuria and still had a garrison in Lushun (Port Arthur). On the other hand, there were many links between China and the USA. Many of China's intellectuals had been educated in

US schools and colleges in China and some had even travelled to the USA. It seemed to many of the intelligentsia who had thrown in their lot with the Communists that the USA represented a more advanced and preferable society to the grim, grey Soviet utopia. Even veterans of the People's Liberation Army (PLA) preferred US weapons to those supplied by their Russian comrades. In practical terms, there were no obvious reasons to clash with the USA. Unlike the Russians, they were not occupying any sovereign Chinese territory and President Truman had made it quite clear that the USA would not defend Chiang Kaishek's refuge in Taiwan.

Perhaps more than the Marxist–Leninist theories that the new Chinese government claimed to subscribe to, it was the weight and tradition of the distant and more recent Chinese past that influenced the new government's conduct of foreign policy. Zhou Enlai and Mao Zedong, like most of their political associates, were part of the May 4th generation (see Chapter 3, page 34). They wanted to see the century-long humiliation of China ended, Chinese territorial integrity restored and foreigners put firmly in their place, which meant putting them outside China. Restoring control over distant Tibet and Xinjiang as the Qing Emperors had done, was part of restoring pride as was carrying the civil war to a final victorious conclusion by occupying Taiwan. Historically, Korea and Vietnam had been tributary states and that relationship should be restored. Mao was very much aware that soon after unifying China in 221 BC Qin Shihuang had sent half a million men to attack Vietnam. Mao sent rather fewer into Korea. The motives were similar: protect the new dynasty from possible attack and show off China's renewed power and strength.

THE ALLIANCE WITH THE USSR

In December 1949, Mao left China for the first time in his life. On 16th December, his train pulled into Moscow and shortly afterwards he was greeted by Stalin and the full Russian Politburo. Stalin welcomed him with the words: 'You are a winner now and winners are always right.' It was meant to break the ice and be friendly, but it hinted at the fact that Stalin had never been that enthusiastic about Mao or the prospects of the Chinese Communist Party (CCP) in seizing power.

Mao had come to Moscow for a range of reasons. At one level, he wanted the blessing of the Marxist–Leninist pope. Stalin was the acknowledged leader of the communist world and Mao could not forget the role Russia and the Comintern had played in the foundation and growth of the Chinese Communist Party (CCP). Mao had out-manoeuvred all the Russian-sponsored candidates for leadership and it would be useful, if not essential, to have Stalin's blessing on his new position as the head of the second most important communist state. More importantly, he wanted help, both military and economic. He hoped for air assistance and special detachments to facilitate the conquest of Taiwan and Tibet. He hoped for a treaty of alliance to protect China from US attack and while gaining cash from the Russians, persuade them to evacuate the areas of China they were still occupying. It was a tall order and Stalin was a formidable negotiator.

In the public sessions such as Stalin's seventieth birthday celebrations, Mao was treated with great respect, but privately he was simply kept hanging around in the comfort of one of Stalin's dachas (houses) outside Moscow. Mao complained bitterly that he had only three things to do – eat, sleep and shit. Stalin was in no hurry and was wary of a communist leader who had come to power largely without Russian assistance. The experience of **Tito** in Yugoslavia was still fresh in his mind. Finally, in early January, Stalin, signalled that Mao should send for Zhou Enlai to begin detailed negotiations. Apparently, the prospect of British recognition of the People's Republic, which occurred on 9th January, led Stalin to act in case Mao should revert to seeking some deal with the west and play off the USSR and the USA.

The treaty that Stalin conceded, which was finally signed on St Valentine's day 1950, was hardly generous. The Treaty of Friendship, Alliance and Mutual Assistance gave China the promise of aid in the event of attack and US$300 million in credits over five years. The USSR promised to evacuate Lushun in 1952. In the meantime, the Soviet Union could shift troops to Lushun when it wished and Russians were to enjoy extra-territorial rights as well as extensive economic concessions in Manchuria and Xinjiang. These latter terms were to be kept secret as

KEY PERSON

(Josip Broz) Tito (1892–1980), the leader of the communist partisans in Yugoslavia during the Second World War, had come to power in 1945, but unlike the other communist leaders of Eastern Europe, imposed by the occupying Russian forces, he owed little to Stalin and in consequence took an independent line that Stalin did not like. In 1948, Stalin began to threaten Tito over his independent relations with the west. Despite Stalin's threats, Tito survived.

Mao and Zhou knew that they infringed Chinese sovereignty and had more than a hint of the hated concessionary treaties of the nineteenth century. Outer Mongolia was to remain ouside Chinese control as a Russian satellite. Stalin gave the Chinese one thing they desired, a list of all the Comintern agents in China, reporting to Moscow. Most were subsequently arrested and many killed.

THE KOREAN WAR

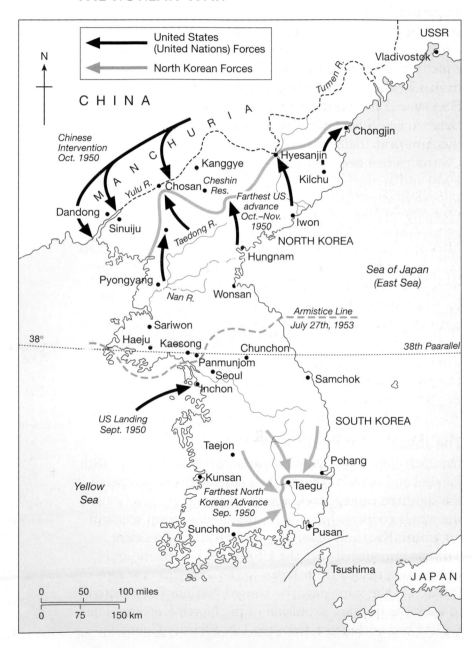

The Korean War, 1950–53

Two months after Mao left Moscow, another Asian communist leader arrived with supplications to the master of the Kremlin. **Kim Il Sung of North Korea** arrived seeking permission to attack the south and reunify the peninsula. In 1949, Stalin had turned down the request, now he agreed and a massive re-equipping of the North Korean army was begun. By June, the north had a considerable superiority over the forces in the south as a result of Soviet generosity – six times as many planes and six and a half times as many armoured vehicles. Stalin argued that international conditions had changed and now favoured the enterprise. In August 1949, the USSR had exploded its own atom bomb, somewhat equalising the power balance with the USA. Furthermore, by January 1950, it seemed increasingly clear that the USA would not defend Korea. The US Secretary of State Dean Acheson had excluded Korea from what he termed the American 'defence perimeter' in the Pacific. The last US troops had been withdrawn from South Korea in 1949 and at the end of January 1950, secret intelligence sources reported that the South Koreans had little hope of US help. The establishment of the People's Republic of China (PRC) also contributed to Stalin's confidence. Mao and the Chinese could always help Kim if things went wrong and thereby avoid a direct US–Soviet confrontation. Kim was told to clear his offensive with Mao. There is nothing to suggest that Mao was initially enthusiastic but assured by the Russians that the USA would not intervene and owing a debt to the Koreans, 100,000 of whom had fought alongside the communist Chinese in Manchuria in 1946–47, Mao assented to a North Korean assault.

The invasion of South Korea

On 25th June 1950, North Korean forces crossed the 38th Parallel and invaded the south. They rapidly seized Seoul, the southern capital, and pressed on to occupy practically the whole country. Initially, it appeared a dream scenario for Stalin, Kim and Mao, but on 27th June, President Truman announced that the USA would intervene and troops were rushed from Japan to the southern port of Pusan. On the same day, the United Nations (UN) voted to back the military expulsion of the North Koreans. The Soviets had withdrawn from the UN Security Council

KEY PERSON

Kim Il Sung of North Korea (1912–) had been a leader of the resistance to the Japanese in the 1930s. In 1941, he fled to Russia and returned with the Soviet armies to Korea in 1945. He became premier of North Korea in 1948 and sought to unify the country in 1950 under his leadership and the dictatorship of the Communist Party.

where they might have vetoed the dispatch of forces to aid the south. The Soviets were loyally supporting their Chinese partners insisting that the Communists assume the UN role for China not the Nationalists of Taiwan. At the same time, as Truman offered aid to South Korea, he reversed US policy with regard to Taiwan, dispatching the US Seventh Fleet to patrol the sea between Taiwan and the Chinese mainland. This was a serious setback to the new communist regime. Prior to this, it only seemed a matter of time before Taiwan was occupied and the PRC gained recognition from the USA and a seat in the Security Council of the United Nations. Throughout the summer, Chinese propaganda emphasised the wickedness of US support for Taiwan more than fighting in Korea. There things got steadily worse. The northern forces became increasingly overstretched and a young Chinese strategist in the PLA correctly guessed the next US move. Kim Il Sung took no advice and when US forces landed at Inchon in September, the North Koreans were completely taken by surprise.

US intervention

This was the scenario that Stalin had not anticipated and Mao had dreaded. As the North Korean army collapsed, Mao was faced with increasingly shrill North Korean appeals for help. The presence of a US satellite Korea bordering Manchuria was deeply worrying to the Chinese. Korea had been Japan's entry into China after 1895. Mao pushed by Kim, Stalin and his own vanity and sense of Chinese history argued for intervention. On 7th October, US forces crossed into what had been North Korea moving from defence to **roll-back.** Many in the Chinese Politburo resisted intervention. China was shattered by years of warfare and the PLA underequipped by western or Russian standards. Lin Biao, possibly China's most brilliant soldier, argued hotly against intervention. Mao later said that there were only one and a half people in favour. He was the one and Zhou Enlai the half. Peng Dehuai joined the discussion late after flying back from Xi'an and threw his weight behind Mao. Mao rightly distrusted Stalin and tried to extract a commitment to supply air power. Stalin was evasive. Eventually, on 13th October, even without a promise of full support, the Chinese resolved to intervene.

KEY TERM

Roll-back meant the attempt not only to restore the *status quo* to June 1950 but also to do what Kim Il Sung had tried to do and unite Korea but under the US-backed Syngman Rhee, whose regime shared many of the attributes of that of Chiang Kaishek.

After a brilliant concealed crossing of the Yalu River, Chinese forces met those of the Republic of Korea (ROK) (South Korea) on 25th October and inflicted a defeat. Over the next few days, they did the same to US forces and then on 6th November, disengaged and withdrew some miles north. It was a brilliant ploy drawing the UN forces into a trap. Instead of retreating as they had thought to do at the beginning of the month, US General Macarthur ordered a pursuit of the retreating Chinese. At the end of November, the Chinese resumed their offensive and over the next few weeks inflicted a catastrophic defeat on the over-extended Americans and South Koreans, driving them out of North Korea and recapturing the southern capital of Seoul. During this period, the US toyed with the use of nuclear weapons to halt the Chinese assault.

China missed a great opportunity to emerge with massively heightened credit from the war by now chasing the dream of total victory in Korea. Peace-feelers were rejected and Peng Dehuai ordered to resume his offensive southwards to complete the final expulsion of the Americans and their allies from Korea. Peng pointed out his difficulties and the appalling suffering of his troops, but to no avail. Stalin was by now supplying limited air cover. The war went on, but now a new US ground commander, General Ridgeway, launched a UN counterattack which pushed the Chinese back north of Seoul. Mao became convinced that total victory was no longer possible and in July 1951, the first armistice negotiations began near to the 38th Parallel. They were to drag on for two years with arguments about exactly where the demarcation line should be and what should happen about the return of prisoners. Stalin seemed content to weaken and embroil the USA and the Americans seemed to be content to keep the Chinese occupied fearing that the ending of hostilities in Korea might lead to the arrival of **Chinese volunteers** in Vietnam. Only after the death of Stalin and the arrival of the new President Eisenhower in the USA, who reflected the US public's growing impatience with the war, was a truce signed on 25th July 1953.

The Korean War was both a triumph and a disaster for China. On the one hand, Chinese troops seemed to have

KEY TERM

Chinese volunteers were part of a pretence that China had not directly intervened and was not declaring war on the USA which might bring massive retaliation to mainland China. The 300,000 troops who crossed the Yalu River in October 1950 were said to have volunteered to fight imperialism.

fought the greatest power in the world to a standstill, perhaps proving Mao's point that the USA was a 'paper tiger'. A friendly North Korea had been preserved on the border of Manchuria where much of China's heavy industry was concentrated. Korea could not so easily be used as a launching ground for attack as it had been by the Japanese. The Russians had been impressed by the fighting qualities of their new allies, which delighted Mao. On the other hand, the cost in lives and precious equipment had been horrendous. Estimates of Chinese casualties vary from something between 400,000 and 800,000. Among them was Mao's son, killed in an air raid on Peng's headquarters. Russia had loaned *matériel* but expected repayment. Most importantly, China had become entrenched in confrontation with the USA, who was now committed to the defence of Taiwan and heavily backing the French in Vietnam to the south. The USA had committed itself to a vast programme of rearmament, and China's prospect of recovering Taiwan and gaining a seat in the Security Council looked hopeless.

CONFRONTING THE USA IN ASIA, 1953–69

Over the next 16 years, US 'imperialism' was the official enemy. China aided North Vietnam in its struggle first with the French and then with the USA in the 1960s. The USA retaliated by trying to subvert Chinese control of Tibet, which had been re-established in 1950. The Americans refused to recognise the PRC and used its influence to exclude it from the UN. A trade embargo was imposed on China on the principle of denying China strategically important goods. (For some reason, this included plastic hair combs, although the proposal to add women's bras was rejected as presumably not having sufficient strategic importance.) To deny China access to dollars, vital in international trade, US citizens were forbidden to buy goods from the PRC. The frigid relationship between the two powers was symbolised by the refusal of the US Secretary of State John Foster Dulles to shake the proffered hand of Zhou Enlai at the Geneva talks on Vietnam in 1954.

The key issue was Taiwan and the survival there of the GMD regime. It was a permanent reminder of the division and weakness of China. In the autumn of 1954, the Chinese chose to emphasise the problem by shelling the islands of Matsu and Quemoy, just off the coast of the mainland and occupied by a large garrison of GMD troops. The USA emphasised its commitment to Taiwan by signing a mutual defence treaty in December 1954. China allowed the bombardment to lapse but asserted her intention to reclaim Taiwan. A fresh crisis arose in 1958 with a renewed bombardment. Mao wished to re-emphasise nationalism at a time of difficulty at home and also sabotage a possible reconciliation between Russia and the west. The day before the crisis began President Eisenhower had invited the Soviets to discuss a test ban treaty on nuclear weapons. The crisis produced much talk of an American nuclear strike on China. But it ended as rapidly as it had begun when on 25th October the Chinese announced that they were suspending bombardment on even days but would continue on odd ones. Clearly, no serious assault on Taiwan was sought, or even conflict with the USA, but China wished to emphasise its continuing claim to total unification and the ending of the GMD regime.

Relations with the USA remained poor all through the 1960s. CIA agents had reputedly encouraged a rising in Tibet in 1959 against Chinese control. It was easily suppressed but fuelled Chinese suspicions, as did the build up of US forces in Vietnam in the 1960s. The Chinese responded with help to the Vietnamese Communists in Hanoi, but of far more importance to Hanoi was the assistance from Russia, and by the 1960s the USSR and the PRC were no longer the allies of the Korean War.

SINO–SOVIET RELATIONS, 1953–69

Mao had always viewed the Soviet Union with a certain suspicion. He had been double-crossed too many times by Stalin. Necessity had, however, driven China firmly into the Soviet camp and the Korean War and subsequent US behaviour kept it there. The Chinese leadership may not have liked Stalin, but they respected him. This was not true of Stalin's successor, Nikita Khrushchev. To Mao, he was a bureaucrat, not a revolutionary comparable to Mao or Stalin. Personally, they did not get on. Ironically, the Russians proved much more generous under Khrushchev than under Stalin. There was generous assistance in promoting China's first Five-Year Plan and thousands of technical experts flooded into China. In 1954, the special rights Russia enjoyed in Xinjiang and Manchuria were ended and on his first visit to Beijing in 1954, Khrushchev offered a much improved trade package compared to the one Stalin had offered in 1950. Furthermore, in 1955, the Russians even promised to help the Chinese build their own atomic bomb and they apparently meant it.

A deteriorating relationship

Perhaps the origins of the worsening relationship lies in Khrushchev's famous denunciation of Stalin in February 1956. It seems to have come as a complete shock to the Chinese delegates and it was not reported in the Chinese press. Mao had had his differences with Stalin but was appalled at the public repudiation of a socialist hero. Likewise, Khruschev's bid for improved relations with Tito and the west excited Mao's contempt. Despite this, Mao was invited to the commemorative celebrations in 1957 of the Russian Revolution. He was treated as an honoured guest and felt a real pride in the Soviet launch of sputnik, naming the first Chinese commune after it on his return. It was in 1958 that relations began to deteriorate seriously. Much to the Russians' surprise, it was two quite innocent requests made to the Chinese that sparked a crisis. The Russians asked to set up a long-wave radio station in China to control a planned Russian Pacific submarine fleet. They also suggested a joint Soviet–Chinese submarine fleet. The suggestions roused all Mao's suspicions and a resentment of being patronised and controlled. Mao demanded that Khrushchev come himself and explain. He agreed to come at once, but the visit was not a success. Here was Mao reflecting the anger of the May 4th generation. He pointed out to his Russian guest:

> The British, Japanese, and other foreigners who stayed in our country for a long time have already been driven away by us. Comrade Khrushchev. I'll repeat it again. We do not want anyone to use our land to achieve their own purposes anymore.

The next day Mao welcomed the Russian leader to his pool and displayed his swimming skills while Khrushchev floundered around with a ring. In the words of Doctor Li, it was Mao's way of 'sticking a needle up his ass'. The Russians were not told of the impending crisis over the off-shore islands, which the Chinese treated as an internal Chinese issue, yet it could embroil the USSR in war with the USA. Mao's seemingly cavalier attitude to nuclear war worried Khrushchev and he was increasingly inclined to regard the Chinese leader as irresponsible and ungrateful.

The ending of the alliance

If relations were showing signs of strain in 1958, it was in 1959 that they broke down. In July, Khrushchev criticised the Great Leap Forward. He had recently had a meeting with Peng Dehuai and the coincidence clearly triggered all Mao's suspicions of Soviet interference in Chinese affairs and that, as in the 1920s and 1930s, the USSR was trying to determine the Chinese Communist leadership. In the summer of 1959, the first clashes occurred on the borders of Tibet and India. The Russians, far from backing China, announced the fighting to be 'sad and stupid'. The Soviet Union extended credits to India. Similarly, in a dispute between China and Indonesia, Russia seemed to favour Indonesia. On August 20th, the final act of betrayal took place when Russia announced to Beijing that it would not be supplying crucial nuclear hardware after all.

A month later Khruschev flew to China for the tenth anniversary of the Chinese Revolution. There was no guard of honour nor even a microphone. Insults were exchanged in private talks, and in a bugged reception room, with only his Russian colleagues, Khrushchev made fun of the Chinese leadership, rhyming their names with obscenities. A new Russian ambassador, appointed at this time, lacked the friendship of Mao that his retiring predecessor had enjoyed. In April 1960, the USSR was openly criticised as revisionist. In the summer of 1960, the Soviet government decided that they would really teach the Chinese a lesson and in the middle of the economic crisis brought on by the Great Leap Forward, withdrew all Russian technicians from China.

Relations in the 1960s continued to deteriorate with rivalry rather than cooperation marking the attitude to the beleaguered North Vietnamese. Mao was increasingly worried by the prospect of a Soviet-sponsored coup against him or even a Russian invasion. The USSR became not only revisionist but imperialist. Part of his suspicions of Liu Shaoqi may have stemmed from Liu's early training in Moscow. There was a very ominous build up of Soviet forces along China's borders. In 1961, there had been only 12 shadow divisions. By 1969, there were 25 full-strength divisions and by 1973, there were 45. The number of Soviet aircraft deployed grew from 200 to 1,200. In 1969, the Soviet newspaper *Pravda* dropped hints of a Russian strike to take out Chinese nuclear capabilities. In March of that year, actual fighting broke out between the Soviet army and the PLA on the Ussuri River which formed the boundary of the two empires. The fighting, although fierce, never escalated into a full-scale conflict. Nevertheless, the Sino–Soviet alliance had collapsed totally.

RECONCILIATION WITH THE WEST, 1969–76

By the end of 1969, many of the conditions making possible a US–Chinese reconciliation were in place. The USA had begun to withdraw troops from Vietnam. There was increasingly a search for a political settlement and in this, China had a crucial part to play. The further development of Chinese oil production, one of the most promising areas of the Chinese economy needed US know-how and skills. Most importantly, Mao worked on the age-old principle that my enemies' enemy is my friend and the deteriorating relationship with the Soviet Union made the USA look increasingly attractive. In 1971 the break-through came. The Chinese government invited the US table-tennis team to Beijing and ping-pong diplomacy was born. In New York, the USA conceded

President Nixon meets Mao, 1972

Chinese membership of the United Nations and in July, Henry Kissinger, the US national security adviser, travelled to China in secret to plan a much more dramatic visit by the impeccably anti-communist president, Richard Nixon.

Nixon's visit in February 1972 shocked the world. Mao, despite his illness and advancing years, was really excited by the prospect of receiving Nixon. Mao had said to his doctor: 'I like to deal with rightists. They say what they really think.' Mao accepted that real problems would still remain but could accept a relationship based on real-politik. Trade relations massively improved, and if formal recognition and the establishment of diplomatic representation did not take place until 1979, there had been a seismic shift to the benefit of both powers. The final US withdrawal from Vietnam in 1973 further eased tensions. Mao also welcomed Prime Minister Tanaka of Japan and apparently struck up a warm personal relationship with him. Both these visits symbolised the new China. The red emperor was receiving suppliants. This was a far cry from the diplomatic dealings of the nineteenth and early twentieth centuries when hostile powers enforced concessions on an enfeebled China.

CHINA AND THE THIRD WORLD

Even when 'leaning to the Soviet side,' China had always tried to play the non-aligned card. Mao's re-interpretation of Marxism, with its theory of a revolutionary peasantry, had an appeal to the less developed nations. Strict Marxist theory demanded a developed capitalist economy before the move to a proletarian revolution. Mao's emphasis on the revolutionary potential of an oppressed peasantry made his branch of Marxism relevant to the undeveloped world and his indictment of imperialism added to his credibility. In Zhou Enlai, Mao had a diplomat of genius, and at Bandung in Indonesia in 1955, Zhou gave China a high profile as one of the leaders of what had been named the Third World. Within the constraints of very limited resources and military power outside her immediate environment, China sought to build on her image as the friend of the poor.

Africa was particularly targeted and by the end of the 1960s, a third of China's embassies were in Africa. As tension developed with the Soviet Union, Mao and Zhou sought to present China as something different and special, the firm opponent of Yankee imperialism but also in the vanguard of those who had seen through Russian deceit and saw the USSR as another oppressive imperialist state. Such an approach brought China friends in the international community but could not make up for the very real poverty which prevented China from competing in the aid stakes with the Soviet Union and even more so with the USA.

CONCLUSION

Much of Chinese foreign policy in these years had been determined by the events of the Korean War. It had locked China into an alliance with the USSR for a decade and made an enemy of the USA for two decades. It ensured China's exclusion from the UN and led the USA to commit itself to the defence of Taiwan, which in 1949 it had had no intention of doing. Eventually, Mao and Zhou, showing a pragmatism which they eschewed at home, escaped from the diplomatic straitjacket that Korea had placed them in. The détente with the USA in the 1970s transformed world diplomatic relations and ultimately enhanced China's standing. It was, however, only really to bear fruit after Mao's death.

SUMMARY QUESTIONS

1 Why did Chinese troops attack UN forces in Korea in October 1950?

2 In what ways did the Korean War affect China's relationship with the USA?

3 Why was there such a serious deterioration in relations between the USSR and the PRC in the years 1956–60?

4 Why did Mao and the PRC decide to invite President Nixon to Beijing and what were the consequences?

TIMELINE	
January 1950	Alliance with USSR
June 1950	North Korea attacks the South
October 1950	China intervenes
1953	Armistice in Korea
1954	Geneva peace talks on Vietnam
1955	Zhou represents China at the Bandung Conference
1956	Khrushchev denounces Stalin in Moscow
1958	Serious clash threatened with USA over offshore islands
1959	Border clash with India
1960	Break with USSR
1969	Border clash with USSR
1971–72	Détente with USA

CHAPTER 12

The last years of the red emperor: China 1969–76

INTRODUCTION

Chinese politics in this period are reminiscent of ancient Rome, or more accurately, ancient China. Mao was more and more inclined to take on the characteristics of his hero, the first Qin Emperor. Marxist–Leninist theory was less a guide to politics than the personal plotting and back-biting that marked an imperial court of 2,000 years before. Wives intrigued on their own and husband's behalf. Failure in this hothouse atmosphere could bring torture and death. Success brought almost unlimited power. **Jiang Qing** talked the language of class struggle and equality. In practice, she behaved like an empress, treating her servants abominably and using her power to pay back real and imagined sleights.

THE TRIUMPH AND FALL OF LIN BIAO, 1969–71

In April 1969, at the Ninth Party Congress, Lin Biao seemed to have ridden the tiger of the Cultural Revolution and emerged triumphant as Mao's nominated heir. The obvious rivals had vanished from the political scene. Liu Shaoqi died that year of deprivation in degrading circumstances. Deng Xiaoping was under arrest in Jiangxi.

Zhou Enlai was still there as number three in the Politburo, but he seems never to have sought the number two slot, still less that of number one, and that is why he had probably survived. His relationship with Lin had always been amicable since they had been together at the Whampoa Military Academy in the 1920s. Number four in the Politburo, Chen Boda, had

> **KEY PERSON**
>
> **Jiang Qing (1914–91)**, generally known as Madame Mao, became one of the most important contenders for power, leading the ultra-left group who were almost more Maoist than Mao. She had played a leading role in launching the Cultural Revolution and identified herself with ideological purity in opposition to pragmatism associated with Deng.

Mao and Lin Biao at the Ninth Party Conference in April 1969

attached himself to Lin's coat tails. Everywhere the People's Liberation Army (PLA) seemed in control and if anyone controlled the PLA, it was Lin Biao. Even his wife, Ye Qun, was a member of the Politburo, a distinction she shared with that other prominent wife, Jiang Qing, also knows as Madame Mao.

Mao was probably the major blot on the horizon. He was 76 years old but still relatively hale and hearty. He was increasingly unpredictable and suspicious. Ye Qun was inclined to be a Mao supporter, surrounding herself with Mao trinkets and quoting extensively from the great man. Despite his public performance of grovelling adulation to Mao, privately Lin Biao did not share his wife's enthusiasm for the Chairman and he detested Madame Mao. The Chairman wielded enormous power but, like the Emperors of old, was often difficult to see and gain an interview with. Even his wife needed to make an appointment. His followers had to guess his purposes from his often obscure utterances. Lin was not as adept at this as Zhou Enlai.

By 1969, there appeared to be three power groupings beneath the enigmatic figure of the Great Helmsman. Lin Biao with a dominant hand over the PLA seemed the most powerful. Jiang Qing and her associates from Shanghai, the future **Gang of Four,** also seemed to enjoy considerable power. Zhou Enlai, still premier, controlled the bureaucracy and was the hope of the senior shattered party cadres. Zhou also enjoyed widespread respect among the intelligentsia.

Lin Biao's power was not as firmly established as it appeared to be. His health was not good. He had a tendency to be a recluse, insisting on spending his time in an atmosphere of exactly 21°C with the blinds drawn to exclude sunlight. Ye Qun was his political manager and seems to have run his office. He was not popular with either the other generals or the surviving old-guard of the party. His closest allies, apart from his wife, were the head of the airforce, Wu Faxian, and Chen Boda. The official Chinese view of the events of 1969–71 which led to Lin Biao's fall and death is that Lin was a scheming rogue trying to consolidate his power as Mao's heir and

KEY TERM

The **Gang of Four** became a well-known phrase in the west in the late 1970s. Its origin lies in a warning from Mao to his wife, in July 1974, against forming 'a Shanghai faction of four'. The other three were Zhang Chunqiao, Wang Hongwen and Yao Wenyuan. Their political power base had been in Shanghai and Mao had used them through his wife as leverage against the more conservative party members in Beijing. They had thus played an important part in launching and later orchestrating the Cultural Revolution. They were regarded as ultra-leftists by the likes of Deng Xiaoping. Wang Hongwen was added to the Politburo in September 1972. Before then, Zhang was the more prominent of the three. Yao Wen yuan was largely a propagandist.

seize the crown. He was, of course, caught out before he could achieve it. In some ways, a more plausible explanation is that he was caught up in a series of palace intrigues, which he was ill-suited to handle, and attracted the deadly and unwarranted suspicion of the aging tyrant. Unlike Peng Dehuai and Liu Shaoqi, he did not go quietly, making self-criticism as instructed, but first tried to defend himself and then fled.

Political hostility and confrontation

Mao seems to have developed a hostility to his new deputy almost as soon as the Ninth Party Congress was over. The dominance of the PLA after the Cultural Revolution aroused his suspicions. 'Why do we have so many soldiers around here?' he kept complaining during a trip to the south in May 1969. His head of security reported to Lin as the next most senior figure in the Politburo. His staff worried that he would catch cold and urged Mao to turn up the heat in his room. He refused. They appealed to Lin who perfectly innocently telephoned Mao to do just this. Lin, as a hypochondriac, would have needed no such urging. Mao was furious, resenting as always attempts to regulate his life. He complained that his staff treated Lin Biao's farts as imperial edicts. Mao was also suspicious that his former political secretary, Chen Boda, seemed to be working rather too closely with the head of the PLA.

These minor irritations grew into a full-scale political confrontation in 1970 over the writing of a new constitution and whether **the position of State President** be revived for Mao to fill. Lin Biao, his wife and Chen Boda all argued that it should. To Mao, this increasingly looked like a manoeuvre to kick him upstairs or install Lin Biao as Vice President as well as Vice Chairman, thus strengthening his position as heir. Either way, Mao was not having it and asked for the matter to be dropped. The Lin clique persisted, thinking that this was the usual false modesty that Mao had often employed in the past. Jiang Qing's clique opposed the new position and encouraged Mao to believe it was part of a plot to strengthen Lin Biao. A bitter faction fight developed at a Central Committee meeting in August 1970 with Chen Boda attacking one of Madame Mao's closest allies. Mao

KEY EVENT

Chen Boda's arrest must have caused consternation to many. Previously, he had been held up by Mao as one of the party's leading theoreticians and was editor of the party journal, *Red Flag*. He was now denounced as a false Marxist. His political destruction together with the subsequent insults heaped on Lin Biao induced a certain cynicism in many of China's young. Some may have begun to reflect that the Great Helmsman seemed to have an unerring talent for picking the wrong candidates.

decided to strike and ordered **Chen Boda's arrest**, Lin Biao's wife made a self-criticism, but Lin himself withdrew into silence fuelling Mao's suspicions.

Over the next few months, Mao began to whittle away at Lin's power base in the PLA, moving his supporters from key positions. Lin could see what was happening and knew well enough the fates of his predecessors, Peng Dehuai and Liu Shaoqi. He laid plans for an escape to Hong Kong if the worst came to the worst. Lin's son with a post in the airforce even began to consider some sort of retaliatory action against Mao, but the plotting does not seem to have been very serious or effective. The plotting of Mao was, however. Lin offended Mao by arriving after him for the May Day celebrations in 1971 and then left without speaking to the Great Helmsman. Mao began to speak regularly of plots to seize power and he moved around the provinces canvassing political provincial leaders.

In the second week of September, Mao suddenly and unexpectedly returned to Beijing. His return triggered a panic reaction on the part of Lin Biao's family. They accelerated their plans to flee. The son commandeered an airforce trident to fly to Canton and then possibly on to Hong Kong. He made the mistake of telling his sister, a Mao loyalist, who was convinced that her father was being kidnapped by her mother and brother. She informed the security forces. A high-speed chase to the airport ensued. Lin and his family reached the jet still in the process of refuelling and at half past midnight with no lights on and the airport in darkness the plane took off. It hit a vehicle and damaged part of the landing gear but managed to become airborne. There was not enough fuel to head south, so they made for the USSR. Without enough fuel, the plane had to attempt a forced landing on the steppes of Mongolia. It crashed killing all the occupants. Mao had lost another successor.

Some western commentators have tried to link Lin Biao's fall and flight to a deep-seated power struggle over foreign policy, and that Lin Biao favoured reconciliation with the USSR and opposed détente with the USA. His fleeing to Russia is seen as confirming this idea. There is little evidence to support such views. He played little

The last years of the red emperor: China 1969–76   161

part in the formulation of foreign policy and seems to have expressed few opinions. The flight to Russia was a last-minute improvisation, the preferred destination being Hong Kong. It is a case of insisting that important events must have important causes. In this case, the downfall of the second most important man in China seems to have grown out of petty court intrigues. Great events can have very trivial causes.

DEATHS AND DEBATE, 1971–76

Mao's health began to deteriorate seriously after the fall of Lin Biao. At an official reception in November 1971 for the North Vietnamese premier, he appeared as a shuffling old man. It was a far cry from the masterful swimmer of 1966. Lung infections exacerbated by years of smoking were affecting his heart. He was a difficult patient, accepting some prescriptions and refusing others. His health was a major political issue, as was the succession.

The flight of Lin Biao strengthened the hands of Jiang Qing who seems to have seen herself in the role of the Dowager Empress Cixi, but there was still Zhou Enlai to contend with. Part of the struggle now turned to the terminology of Lin's treason. Was he a dangerous leftist, as Zhou Enlai implied, and therefore his downfall would clear the way for a rehabilitation of some of the victims of the Cultural Revolution? Was he a repressive rightist and therefore his removal cleared the path for Jiang Qing and her Shanghai gang?

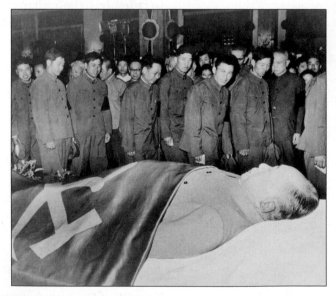

Remains of Chairman Mao in Great Hall of the People.

As usual, Mao gave out conflicting signals. In December 1972, he agreed with his wife that Lin had been an ultra-rightist and revisionist. On the other hand, in a development deeply worrying to Jiang Qing he agreed to bring Deng Xiaoping back to the land of the politically living. In February 1973, Deng left Jiangxi and returned to Beijing as vice premier under Zhou Enlai. Deng brought administrative ability and experience, both in short supply since the purges of the Cultural Revolution. He had prestige in the party, whose morale Mao now wanted to restore, and he had prestige in the PLA. The eight regional commanders had developed too much power and Mao had no wish to see a return to the era of the warlords on his death. Deng was also eventually appointed chief of staff of the army. Mao was hoping to keep a balance between the pragmatists and the supporters of the Cultural Revolution. At the same time as Deng's recall, Wang Hongwen was summoned from Shanghai and added to the Politburo, possibly as a future successor. Mao was determined that the old pragmatic revisionists would not have it all their own way. To rub in the point, an **Anti-Confucius campaign** began in 1973. It was clearly aimed at Zhou Enlai. Another relative youngster, Hua Guafeng, was brought from Mao's native Hunan and given Politburo status. The Tenth Party Congress of 1973 rubber stamped the uneasy balance between the factions. Mao appeared to be creating a new generation of leaders and there was need.

Chen Boda was in prison, Kang Sheng was dying of cancer and Zhou Enlai had just been diagnosed with it in the spring of 1973. Mao himself was fragile and, in July 1974, was diagnosed with a rare motor neurone disease which would kill him in a couple of years. The faction fighting intensified. Should examinations be used to determine entrance to university as schools and colleges reopened after the Cultural Revolution? The radicals led by Jiang Qing argued that class background was more important than academic attainment and there should be no examinations as these favoured the traditional elite. Two individual cases were used as propaganda by the radicals against the existing entrance system to university. Student Zhang had been too busy in a production team, working 18 hours a day, to do any studying and handed in a blank sheet in examination. The radicals argued that such 'revolutionary purity' was more important than book knowledge. Student Zhang resigned his university place

KEY EVENT

The **Anti-Confucius campaign** was on the surface a literary/historical debate about the persecution of Confucian scholars by the first Qin Emperor. The line pushed by the radicals, obviously with Mao's support, was that the Qin Emperor was being progressive to persecute essentially backward looking supporters of Confucius. All the intelligentsia realised that the Confucian scholars were a metaphor for Zhou Enlai and his supporters in the bureaucracy.

having gained admission via backstairs influence, feeling guilty as the beneficiary of favouritism. The pragmatists wanted some proof of merit. There were similar arguments with regard to industry, with Deng favouring payment related to effort and the radicals stressing that equality was more important and selfishness at all costs should be discouraged. Coming from Jiang Qing, this was rather ironic in view of her utterly selfish and self-indulgent behaviour with her own staff.

Jiang Qing and her allies tried to whip up the Anti-Confucius campaign to bring down Deng and Zhou. Wang Hongwen had proved a disappointment, easily outclassed by Deng and driven into lowly dependence on Jiang Qing, who increasingly irritated Mao. He denounced her at a Politburo meeting 'as representing only herself'. It was on this occasion that the Gang of Four were born as a concept. Deng Xiaoping's stock continued to rise and, in October 1974, he was appointed vice premier, in effect Zhou Enlai's successor. He was increasingly handling important foreign policy issues with his usual skill. Mao decided at the end of the year to make him a vice chairman of the Central Committee and vice chairman of the military commission. Deng was appointed to these in January 1975. He now, in effect, held positions of authority in all of the central bodies governing the Chinese state – party, army and government bureaucracy. The pragmatists seemed to have won. Mao, however, might be ill but he was not dead yet.

Late in 1975, **Deng lost Mao's confidence** again. Mao became convinced that the ex-capitalist roadster was up to his old tricks and had forgotten the primacy of class struggle in his bid for stability and economic growth. He lost some of his positions but still had an oversight of foreign policy. When Zhou Enlai died in January, it was Deng who gave the official speech. Events in April, however, further damaged him and brought about his second removal from office. From the end of March, there appears to have been a popular upsurge of feeling for Zhou Enlai and against Madame Mao. Poems and posters attacked the 'Mad Empress' and her supporters and expressed sorrow and honour for Zhou. These reached a climax on 4th April during the Qingming Festival,

KEY EVENT

Deng lost Mao's confidence Mao seems to have tested Deng on his genuine conversion to Mao's values by asking him to chair a Politburo evaluation of the Cultural Revolution with the clear direction to make a positive judgement. Deng argued that as he was not around at the time, he was an inappropriate person to carry out the evaluation. He further upset Mao by backing the removal of two radicals from Qinghua University. Clearly, he still felt that the colour of the cat didn't matter. To Mao, the colour was all important.

traditionally associated with paying respect to parents and ancestors. Tiananmen Square was covered in tributes to Zhou. Some placards announced that the reign of the Qin Emperor was now over. The Anti-Confucian campaign had backfired. At night, the wreaths and tributes were removed by the authorities. The next day an angry crowd of 100,000 filled the square demanding the tributes be returned. Scuffles broke out with police. Security forces finally cleared the square and made extensive arrests. Mao and the Politburo announced that it was a revisionist and counter-revolutionary event. Deng was stripped of all his posts and Hua Guafeng appointed vice chairman of the party and premier in succession to Zhou. Here was Mao's successor.

Deng simply escaped this time. He refused to make any self-criticism or wait for his arrest. With the help of the military commander in the Canton region, he flew south and remained in hiding till Mao was dead. Mao clearly could not live much longer. Beginning on 12th May, he suffered the first in a series of heart attacks. His former military comrade Zhu De died on 6th July, and in the same month, nature, in the traditional fashion, announced the death of the emperor with an horrific earthquake, 100 miles from Beijing. At least a quarter of a million people died, with many times that number injured. On 9th September 1976, Mao finally gave up the struggle to live. The reign of the Qin Emperor was over as the placards of April had predicted.

THE SUCCESSION

Hua Guafeng succeeded to all the top positions. He became chairman of the Central Committee and chairman of the military commission, while still retaining the premiership. For all his official positions, he lacked real status in his own right and when attacked by the Gang of Four turned to the senior army bosses for help. The senior serving marshal, Ye Jianying, and the head of Mao's personal security detachment came to his aid and on the night of 6th October arrested the Gang of Four in a skilful and secretive coup. Their leading supporters followed them into prison. The Cultural Revolution was finally over and the way cleared for Deng's return to the front line. This happened in the summer of 1977. The pragmatists had won.

Over the next three years, Deng gently eased Hua from power and, in 1980, from office. Over the next 20 years, it became abundantly clear that catching mice was what mattered and not the colour of the cat. As the living standards of the Chinese people rose dramatically, most came to agree with Deng regarding the colour of the cat. Jiang Qing had once argued the converse with a different metaphor: 'Better a socialist train that arrives late than a capitalist train on time.' By 1981, Jiang Qing was facing life in prison, Deng was the new emperor and the capitalist train was arriving on time. Her brand of socialism was increasingly a nightmare from the past.

ASSESSMENT OF THE NEW DYNASTY, 1949–76

As a leading American academic, Samuel Huntington, argued:

> *Surely one of the most outstanding achievements of the mid-twentieth century was the establishment in China in 1949 for the first time in a hundred years of a government really able to govern China.*

This was a major success after years of anarchy and disunity. Mao's regime did what Chiang Kaishek had tried to do and it exercised an authority unseen since the Qianlong emperor in the eighteenth century.

In addition, it had raised the self-respect of Chinese citizens with regard to the rest of the world. The national humiliations which fuelled the anger of the May 4th generation had been replaced by a new pride and self-confidence. Foreigners were once again few and knew their place as in the days of the Qianlong emperor. China was a member of the select nuclear club by 1964. China had reasserted her prestige in the traditionally tributary states of Korea and Vietnam, in the process producing setbacks to the greatest power in the world. The leader of that great power had actually come to China and treated Mao, as the ruler of China with considerable deference and respect in the 1970s. It was a far cry from the treaties forced on China in the nineteenth and early twentieth centuries.

Within China some of the May 4th agenda had been achieved. Women had certainly benefited and, in theory at least, had gained equality. Opium, the curse of the nineteenth century, had been much reduced as a social problem. Literacy and access to education had been extended considerably. By 1976, 96 per cent of children were attending primary schools. Only 30 per cent of males had been literate in the early twentieth century and the figure was much lower for females. By the mid-1970s, there were a million barefoot doctors bringing some kind of medical care to areas which had never known it. Heavy industry had continued to develop in Manchuria and mining and oil extraction had made great strides in some regions.

On the other side of the ledger, if order had been restored, law had not. An arbitrary government interfered at will with the persons and property of Chinese citizens. Human rights as understood in the west were not respected. Without that sanctity of law and the security it brought, further economic development would be difficult. Millions had been shot, imprisoned, tortured or directed to some rural hell hole to rot. Millions had starved to death in the greatest famine of human history. Had Mao died in 1956, his achievements would undoubtedly be seen as outweighing his demerits, but he was to live and rule for another 20 years, writing on what he claimed was the blank page of Chinese society.

With the Hundred Flowers campaign of 1957, he first raised then dashed the hopes of China's intellectuals stamping firmly on freedom of expression. With the introduction of communes, he alienated the peasants and in the Great Leap Forward condemned millions to a lingering death through starvation. The pursuit of equality and the defence of his personal power produced the mass frenzy of the Cultural Revolution, casting China back into the chaos that communist victory in 1949 seemed to have banished. A vicious and unresolved power struggle marked the last years.

CONCLUSION

Mao had enjoyed writing on the blank page of Chinese society, but whether the writing was the beautiful calligraphy he talked of is open to debate. The official Chinese verdict pronounced by the Central Committee in 1981 was that Mao had been 70 per cent correct and 30 per cent mistaken, the mistakes coming mainly towards the end of his life. It was a judgement that was almost inevitable, for the Communist Party could not condemn its Chairman without fatally undermining its own legitimacy. But, in the last resort, it is not as a Communist that Mao should be viewed. The man who declared war on old culture was himself the living embodiment of the power of old culture. He was the Buddhist Monkey King and the Qin Emperor returned to both liberate and oppress this ancient civilisation.

SUMMARY QUESTIONS

1 Account for the fall of Lin Biao in September 1971.

2 Why were the years 1971–76 marked by bitter factional strife among the leadership of the People's Republic?

3 In what ways did Mao Zedong control his political colleagues in the years 1971–76?

4 In what ways might the People's Republic be considered a success by 1976?

TIMELINE

1969	Ninth Party Congress appoints Lin Biao as Mao's successor
1970	Issue of State Presidency debated
1971	Flight and death of Lin Biao
1973	Deng Xiaoping re-appointed; Anti-Confucian campaign
1974	Mao diagnosed as terminally ill
December 1975	Deng loses some power
January 1976	Death of Zhou Enlai
April 1976	Dismissal of Deng
Sept 1976	Death of Mao
October 1976	Arrest of Gang of Four

AS ASSESSMENT

There are four types of questions set in the Edexcel China options.

1). **China under Mao 1949–76** is a Unit 2 Option and there are two pairs of questions, from which candidates answer one pair. It is not possible to mix and match. Candidates must answer 1a and 1b or 2a and 2b NOT 1a and 2b.

The question invites a short focused description and is worth 20 marks. The question stems could be "describe the role"; "describe the key features of"; "in what ways did"; "by what stages did". The response should take 15–20 minutes and cannot in consequence be much longer than one side in length.

Sample question:

> In what ways did the new communist government of China seek to improve the status of women in China?

The topic is covered on page 95 of this book. A suitable response would be –

> The key development was the New Marriage Law of 1950. Women traditionally in China had been subject to arranged marriages and thereafter bound to the service of the groom's family before their own. Divorce was difficult for women and their property rights insecure. Amongst the richer families of the ruling elite, wives shared their husbands with concubines, in effect lower status wives kept for the sexual gratification of the wealthy male. The marriage law removed many of these grievances. Arranged marriages were forbidden as were dowries, without which in the past many girls could not find a husband. Women were to have equal rights to property and divorce was to be available on equal terms. In one sense women's divorce rights were superior to men's as a male could not now divorce his pregnant wife nor for a year after the birth of the child. The law outlawed the keeping of concubines.

> How far and how quickly this law came to be applied is open to doubt. Concubines might be illegal but even Chairman Mao had several attendant girlfriends in addition to his formidable fourth wife. Despite this there is little doubt that the law did much to mark a major improvement in the lives of Chinese women and was the central plank in the new government's attempts to raise the status of women.

The new China also gave women a higher profile in terms of work and education. There was an increase in the numbers attending schools and universities and increasing job opportunities in the expanding party bureaucracy. The assault on prostitution which had been widespread slowly reduced the number of brothels in the 1950s and might be seen as raising the status of women. On the other hand it might be seen as curbing their economic freedom.

The b) question invites a causal analysis and is worth 40 marks. Candidates should spend approximately 35–40 minutes responding. The answer should be multi-causal and not stray into superfluous narrative. To achieve the highest mark, candidates should be able to demonstrate the interaction of causes i.e. how one line of causation intertwines and relates to another or many others. A hierarchy of the importance of the causes might be shown although this is not explicitly demanded. Most answers will be two sides in length.

Sample question:

Why was the Cultural Revolution started in the summer of 1966?

A suitable response might be:

In May 1966 the politburo approved a circular explaining that counter-revolutionary revisionists who were representatives of the bourgeoisie had sneaked into the party. They needed to be exposed. The first red guard unites were formed at Qinghua University at the end of the month to expose these "snakes" and mass red guard rallies were held in August. The Cultural Revolution had begun. Ostensibly it was to purge a corrupt party and it appeared to aim to do this through the mass participation of the young. The one question already becomes two questions. Why did the politburo want to purge the party and why did the young join in the task with such enthusiasm.

The issuing of the politburo circular was the climax of a long power struggle which had been going on since 1962. It represented two different approaches to putting right what had gone wrong with the Great Leap Forward. Mao wanted to root out corruption and half-heartedness by turning to mass mobilisation. More socialism not less had to be inculcated into the party. Liu Shaoqi, Deng Xiaoping and the senior party bureaucrats wanted rectification from above and the weeding out of corruption and incompetence. By the issuing of this circular Mao appeared to have got his way and defeated Deng and Liu. It was not however just a product of an argument about how to proceed or the degree of socialism although this was important. Arguments over policy had become a clash of personalities and personal jealousies intertwined with an ideological clash. Mao had become jealous of Liu, now head of state and a rival to Mao as head of the party. Mao felt slighted and determined to recentralise himself as the one source of authority. Events in Russia had raised Mao's suspicions of his colleagues. In Russia Khrushchev had been deprived by his colleagues after a series of failures and bungles, none of which were in the same league of disasters as Mao's Great Leap Forward. The Soviet defence minister had urged a Chinese general to get rid of their "clown" just as the Russians had got rid of Khrushchev. Mao was determined to preserve his position and if Liu was the Chinese Breshnev the masses would deal with him.

It was not however Mao alone that launched the Cultural Revolution. He needed allies, most notable being Lin Biao, head of the PLA and Mao's own wife, Jiang Qing. Others in the politburo like Chen Boda, the ideological chief and Kang Sheng, the security chief were happy to oblige the chairman. As with Mao, personal and political motives intermingled. Madam Mao was jealous of the elegant and sophisticated wife of Liu Shoqui. Both Liu and Deng dominated the party hierarchy and seemed to block the path of Lin, Chen and Kang. There was also no doubt that madam Mao and the others sympathised with Mao's ideological purity and felt that Liu and Deng had retreated too far from socialism in the aftermath of the Great Leap Forward. They did not agree with Deng that the colour of the cat did not matter as long as it caught mice. The cat should be red. So at one level the Cultural Revolution was a power struggle among the upper reaches of the Chinese communist party over policy and position.

Why there was such mass hysterical support for the Cultural Revolution is explained by a complex mix of motives. Jealousy of senior colleagues and the prospect of promotion if they were removed motivated many junior party officials. To many students and children it was simply exciting. In the highly regimented and disciplined society of communist China, suddenly to be told to attack figures of authority by the ultimate figure of authority was too good an opportunity to be missed. Unpopular teachers could be tortured and killed. The houses of the slightly well off could be looted and all in the name of Mao and building a beautiful new utopia. The Cultural Revolution as an event involving mass *participation is reminiscent of several previous Chinese popular explosions, the Boxer rising of 1900, and the Taiping rebellion of the 1860s. It was the periodic blowing of a valve in this highly controlled environment. In this case the man who released the pressure was undoubtedly Mao and the chief cause therefore of the Cultural Revolution was his resentment of his senior colleagues.*

The timing of the release was determined by the interplay of many factors. Not least the time it took for Mao to put his pieces into place after the setbacks he suffered in 1962. The build-up of Lin Biao's grip on the PLA and its radicalisation took time as did that of Madam Mao in the world of the arts. Mao's resentment of his colleagues since 1962 was increased by the fall of Khrushchev in 1964 and again in January 1965 by the high profile re-election of Liu Shaoqi as state president. A complex and devious plot to undermine Liu Shaoqi then developed involving an attack on a young playwright who Mao felt had indirectly criticised him. First the playwright was slowly brought to book then his friend and protector, Peng Zhen, the Mayor of Beijing, a key ally of Liu, and finally when Peng was pushed out in the spring of 1966 and Mao's hold on the capital was more secure, the main assault could be launched. Many threads would come together to produce the launch of the Cultural Revolution but one man united the threads, Mao.

2). **China circa 1900–49** is to be found in Unit 3 and once again candidates face two pairs of questions. The first will be for 20 marks and could be a "describe" question as in unit 2 or a "why" question. If it is a "why" question, clearly it cannot elicit the same length of answer as a 40 mark unit 2 question. A mere 15 minutes should be devoted to answering, which means one side at the most. If there is a date in the question, this should be addressed.

<u>Example</u>

Why did the Qing dynasty lose the imperial throne in 1912?

A suitable response might be:

The emperor in 1912 was a child and in no position to control events. Imperial authority had been in decline for several decades. The previous emperor had been under house arrest for 11 years and power had been exercised by the formidable Dowager Empress. On her death in 1908, no one figure in the Imperial family exercised effective authority.

Resentment of the Qing Dynasty had been growing for decades, amongst the native Han Chinese. The Qing had failed to prevent the repeated humiliation of China by foreign powers. They accepted the huge compensation accorded to the Western Powers following the Boxer Rising. Large numbers of the ruling scholar elite accepted that reforms had to be carried through as they had been in Japan following the Meji Revolution of 1867. The Qing failed to give a lead until it was too late. The Dowager Empress first rejected reform then just before her death embraced reform in a flood of decrees which destabilised the situation further. Power was increasingly slipping away to provincial governors, who kept most of the revenue from land taxes.

Ideas of revolution and reform were spreading amongst the educated young who looked to Sun Yatsen and the Revolutionary alliance for leadership. It was amongst the students that revolution was to begin. Nature added an ingredient with torrential rain in 1910 and 1911, producing widespread floods and rising grain prices. The final trigger to revolt was a decision by the Qing government to take over provincial run railway companies with minimal compensation. Gentry, local officials and student activists united and riots broke out and spread in the summer of 1911. The vast western province of Sichuan was lost by September. The final explosion began in Wuchang, the great tri-city of the central Yangtse. Many provincial armies mutinied and by the end of the year, the Manchu regime in Beijing had lost control of most of the country. Sun Yatsen returned from exile to Nanjing, where he was elected President of a new China. The mother of the young emperor decided to cut her losses and negotiate a generous abdication settlement in February 1912.

Weakness at the centre combined with growing resentment at many levels of society had combined to topple the 250 year old dynasty.

The b) question, worth 40 marks, invites a value judgement, usually on causes or consequences. It often asks 'How far one factor was responsible for an outcome. In this case the correct approach is to address the stated factor and then weigh it against other causes and so reach a judgement. A short conclusion should always be included.

Example:

How far was the Communist victory in the Civil War of 1946–49 a result of Soviet aid and assistance?

This is of course dealt with in chapter 6, particularly the last section.

A suitable response might be:

It is sometimes asserted that Mao and his Communist forces owed their victory in the Civil War to help from Moscow. Mao's red army in China in 1945 was nearly a million strong but weak in artillery and almost totally without air-power. The Soviet Union's biggest contribution to their victory was the handing over to the Communists of large quantities of captured Japanese munitions in Manchuria, taken from the arsenal at Shenyang. Previously the Chinese Communists had only 600 artillery pieces. They now gained several thousand, courtesy of Stalin. In addition they were allowed to establish themselves in Manchuria by the occupying Soviet forces before the Soviets withdrew. Manchuria was to prove the decisive area of conflict and thus the Soviet aid was not negligible. On the other hand, there was no direct Soviet intervention and aid was less in total than that provided to the Nationalists by the USA .Throughout much of the conflict Soviet help was half-hearted and advice often positively harmful. They ordered the Chinese Communists to withdraw from the Manchurian cities in 1946 and advised them not to cross the Yangtse in 1949 in order to finish off the Chiang regime, which the Russians almost appeared to be seeking to preserve. (Stated factor dealt with and weighed in this paragraph)

The Communists enjoyed many other advantages which help to explain their victory. They were able to attract a broad spectrum of support. Their armies deliberately tried to win over the peasantry by avoiding the usual brutal behaviour that soldiers meted out to the farming community. In Manchuria, they seem to have been effective in building rural bases of support and in the great battle of Xuzhou which lasted 65 days, Deng Xiaoping was able to mobilise the support of 2 million peasant labourers to provide logistical support to the armies of Zhu De. Middle class intellectuals increasingly came over to the Communists as the genuine heirs of the May 4th movement. The Communist armies were also disciplined and well led. Lin Biao proved an outstanding commander in the Manchurian fighting of 1947–48. Mao, in contrast to Chiang seems to have trusted his subordinates and delegated effectively. The Communists also enjoyed superior intelligence, having penetrated the Nationalist military command at the highest level.

The weaknesses of the Nationalists also explain their defeat. Rampant inflation eroded support from the urban middle classes who were the bedrock of the nationalist regime. Absentee landlords, many of them officers in the Nationalist armies failed to exert influence on the rural bulk of China, which increasingly passed under Communist control. Corruption in the Nationalist armies was rampant as American observers pointed out and Chiang preferred loyalty to competence in his appointment of subordinates. In the end the war was lost as a result of a series of military blunders on Chiang's part. He chose to fight his major campaign in Manchuria, far from his areas of bedrock support. A vast percentage of his military budget went into trying to supply his beleaguered armies far to the north. Much of his superior air-power went into the same futile strategy. In 1948, he lost Manchuria and half a million of his best troops. Instead of regrouping and husbanding his resources for a decisive battle in his Yangtze stronghold, he made another stubborn and disastrous defence in the south of Shandong province. In other words the war was lost as a result of military incompetence.

Help from the Soviet Union, played a part in the Communist victory, particularly the supplying of artillery from captured Japanese supplies in 1945–46. This did not prevent the Communist defeats in 1946–47. The Communist victories of 1948–49 were largely a result of other factors, not least the military incompetence of Chiang.(short but focussed conclusion)

BIBLIOGRAPHY

GENERAL TEXTS ON CHINESE HISTORY
Dawson, R (1978) *The Chinese Experience*, Weidenfeld & Nicolson.

Gasgoigne, B (1973) *The Dynasties of China*, Jonathan Cape.

Hook, B (ed.) (1991) *The Cambridge Encyclopedia of China*, Cambridge University Press.

Roberts, J A G (1999) *A History of China*, Macmillan.

TEXTS ON MODERN CHINA
Jenner, W J F (1992) *The Tyranny of History: The Roots of China's Crisis*, Allen Lane.

Mitter, R (2004) *A Bitter Revolution: China's Struggle with the Modern World*, Oxford.

Schoppa, R K (2000) *The Columbia Guide to Modern Chinese History*, Columbia Press.

Spence, J D (1999) *The Search for Modern China*, Norton.

Twitchett, D and J K Fairbank (eds) (1978–91) *The Cambridge History of China*, vols 10–15, Cambridge University Press. (Covers the period 1800–1982)

BIOGRAPHIES
Evans, R (1991) Deng Xiaoping and the Making of Modern China, Oxford University Press.

Fenby, J (2003) *Generalissimo: Chiang Kai-Shek and the China He Lost*, The Free Press.

Teiwes, F C and W Sun (1996) *The Tragedy of Lin Biao*, Hurst.

MAO IN DESCENDING ORDER OF APPROVAL OF THEIR SUBJECT
Schram, S (1966) *Mao Tse Tung*, Penguin.

Short, P. (1999) *Mao: A Life*, John Murray.

Jung Chang and J Halliday (2005) *Mao: The Untold Story*, Jonathan Cape.

MEMOIRS
Cheng Nien (1986) *Life and Death in Shanghai*, Grove Press.

Gao Yuan (1987) *Born Red: A Chronicle of the Cultural Revolution*, Stanford University Press.

Jung Chang (1991) *Wild Swans: Three Daughters of China*, Harper Collins.

Terrill, R (1992) *China in Our Time*, Touchstone.

Zhang Xianliang (1994) *Grass Soup*, Secker & Warburg.

Zhisui Li (1994) *The Private Life of Chairman Mao*, Chatto and Windus.

INDEX

Headings in italics refer to publications, etc. Page numbers in italics refer to illustrations or maps.